2024 CONSUMER TREND INSIGHTS

First published in the Republic of Korea in November, 2023 by Miraebook Publishing Co.

Inquiries should be addressed to
Miraebook Publishing Co.
5th Fl., Miraeui-chang Bldg., 62-1 Jandari-ro, Mapo-ku, Seoul
Tel : 82-2-325-7556 / email : ask@miraebook.co.kr

www.miraebook.co.kr
blog.naver.com/miraebookjoa
Instagram.com/miraebook
Facebook.com/miraebook

ISBN 978 89 5989 720 9 13320

2024
CONSUMER
TREND
INSIGHTS

Rando Kim · Miyoung Jeon · Jihye Choi · Soojin Lee ·
Jung Yoon Kwon · Dahye Han · June Young Lee · Hyang Eun Lee ·
Hyewon Lee · Yelin Chu · Dahyen Jeon · Proofread by Michel Lamblin

미래의 창

Authors

Rando Kim (김난도)

Rando Kim is a professor in the Dept. of Consumer Science (DCS), Seoul National University (SNU). As a specialist in consumer behavior and market trend analysis, he has written more than 20 books including *Trend Korea* series, *Dining Business Trend* series, *Market Kurly Insight, The Hyundai Seoul Insight, Trend China, What Consumers Want,* and *Luxury Korea.* He also wrote essay books, *Amor Fati, Future and My Job,* and *Youth, It's Painful* which is sold three million copies in 17 countries. He has conducted research projects about consumer needs finding, new product planning, and market trend probing for Korea's major companies like Samsung, LG, SK, CJ, Hyundai Motors, GS, LH, Amore Pacific, Lotte, Fursys, Nongshim, and Coway.

Miyoung Jeon (전미영)

Miyoung Jeon is a research fellow at the Consumer Trend Center (CTC) under Seoul National University. She holds BA, MA and PhD degrees in Consumer Science. Since 2009, she has co-authored numerous books including the annually published and top-ranked book series *Trend Korea* series, as well as *Trend China, Dining Business Trend* series, and *Breakthrough Power.* Miyoung worked as a research analyst at Samsung Economic Research Institute, served as a research professor at SNU, and is currently a columnist for *Dong-A Ilbo's* 'Trend Now' section. Additionally, she holds positions as the chair for Lotte Shopping's ESG Committee and serves as an advisor for multiple organizations including LG U+, Hana Bank and the Seoul Metropolitan Government. Currently, she collaborates with various companies, focusing on new trend-based product development and strategic planning.

Jihye Choi (최지혜)

Jihye Choi, PhD in Consumer Science from DCS, SNU, works as a research fellow at CTC. She has participated in many consulting projects with Korea's leading companies such as Samsung and LG, and gives public lectures on consumer trends. She currently teaches consumer behavior and qualitative research methodology at SNU. She contributes many articles and columns to major Korean newspapers and media.

Soojin Lee (이수진)

Soojin Lee earned a doctorate degree in Consumer Science from SNU and currently works as a research fellow at CTC. Prior to joining the center, she was a stock market reporter *on Maeil Economic TV*. As a contributing researcher, she is conducting a number of consulting projects with Korea's major companies such as Samsung and LG, and received 'The Best Publication Award' from the Korean Academic Society of Financial Planning in 2018. Also, as a lecturer she teaches consumer culture and consumer psychology at SNU.

Jung Yoon Kwon (권정윤)

Jung Yoon Kwon currently works as a research fellow at CTC, SNU. She obtained her BA, MA, and PhD degrees in Consumer Science, SNU. She explored the intergenerational transmission of consumption styles in her

PhD dissertation. She has participated in many consulting projects with leading Korean companies such as Samsung and CJ, and she also teaches an introduction to Consumer Science at Sung Kyun Kwan university.

Dahye Han (한다혜)

Dahye Han currently works as a research fellow at CTC, SNU. She received a BA in Psychology, SNU and obtained MA and PhD degrees in Consumer Science, SNU. Her PhD dissertation focused on the structure and measurement of consumption emotions. As a researcher, she received a paper award from the Korean Consumption Culture Association in 2022. Also, she is conducting a number of consulting projects with major Korean companies, such as Samsung and LG.

June Young Lee (이준영)

June Young Lee currently works as a professor at Sangmyung University. He received a doctorate degree in Consumer Science, SNU. He received 'The Best Paper Award' *in the International Journal of Consumer Studies*. He worked as a senior researcher at Life Soft Research lab at LG Electronics. He is a laboratory chief at the Consumer Research Center in Sangmyung University.

Hyang Eun Lee (이향은)

Hyang Eun Lee is a Vice President of LG Electronics, H&A Customer eXperience (CX) Division, and an associate professor in the Dept. of Service Design Engineering at Sungshin Women's University. While being a corporate professional and a professor, she co-authored numerous trend insight books and is a renowned columnist for *JoongAng Ilbo*. She received a PhD in Design from the Graduate School of Arts, SNU, and a master's degree in Design Management from Central Saint Martins in London, England.

Hyewon Lee (이혜원)

Hyewon Lee, a PhD candidate in Consumer Science, SNU and is currently a senior researcher at CTC. She is interested in generation theory and changes in consumer behavior due to technological advances, based on insights gained while working at the Korea Publishing Culture Association, Dasan Books, Reader's Book, and Kakao Page. Recently, she has been conducting research on expanded cultural capital to explore the drivers of consumption trends that cannot be explained by economic capital.

Yelin Chu (추예린)

Yelin Chu received an MA degree in Consumer Science, SNU. Currently, she is attending a PhD program and serves as a senior researcher at CTC. Her Master's thesis was entitled "A Study of Consumer Experience on the Online Education Service with Conditional Tuition Refund." She is interested in analyzing big data to distill insights from unstructured data, and in deriving further meaning from participant interviews through qualitative research.

Dahyen Jeon (전다현)

Dahyen Jeon is currently working on her PhD and is a senior researcher at CTC. She received a BA degree in Fashion Industry at Ewha Womans University and an MA degree in Consumer Science at SNU. She was awarded first place in the Korean Society of Clothing and Textiles (KSCT) contest in 2019. Her area of interest is consumer behavior in the digital retail environment. Her current research focuses on online visual cues and haptic imagery.

DRAGON EYES
The era of artificial intelligence, ultimately, is human

"ChatGPT, tell us about Korea's consumer trends in 2024."

It was the evening that the top ten consumer trend keywords for this book were finalized through a comprehensive workshop with "Trenders Nal트렌더스 날," a trend hunter group that has been in operation for over 17 years, after three weeks of brainstorming by the *Trend Korea* team. We asked ChatGPT what trends will be forecasted for 2024. I was curious how different our outlook would be from AI's analysis.

1. Sustainable consumption

2. Strengthening digital experiences

3. Increased interest in health and well-being

4. Customized products and personalization

5. Emphasis on local and regional experiences

6. Post-pandemic trends

7. Expansion of social media shopping

8. Introduction of robots and automation technology

These are the top eight trends selected by ChatGPT. They're quite plausible. As we delved deeper into our inquiries, we engaged in our own prompt engineering to obtain more sophisticated and detailed explanations. However, fundamentally, AI did not stray from the scope of the initial eight trends.

How can we evaluate these trends? Of course, they are not incorrect. Everything is headed in the right direction. But here's something to ponder: Can AI compose a nearly 300-page book centered around these eight trends? Quantity-wise, it might manage to do so. But can we generate examples and logical explanations that would captivate readers from start to finish? Even if our writing team puts in considerable effort to create a manuscript utilizing the eight trends mentioned above, will readers still embrace the book, knowing how the trends were generated?

As the author of a consumer trends series of books, my initial reaction upon seeing the trends generated by AI was one of relief. This feeling stemmed from the confirmation that there remains a portion of creativity – perhaps more than 2%, or even as much as 20% – that AI cannot replicate. The same sentiment applied to the illustrations as well.

Given that 2024 is the Year of the Dragon, we decided to incorporate a dragon design into the merchandise for readers who pre-order the book. I was able to obtain an intricately crafted dragon illustration using BlueWillow, an AI image generator. However, the image it produced felt unsettling, and I ultimately couldn't use it. Unlike in the East, where dragons are revered as auspicious spirits, Western culture often portrays dragons as fierce and malevolent beings. It's possible that the AI trained on this perspective, which could explain the unsettling result. In the end, we turned to a professional human illustrator who was able to create a dragon drawing that met our standards and captured the essence of 2024, the Year of the Blue Dragon.

The *Trend Korea* series has also been published in English as *Consumer Trend Insights* since 2020. Because the preliminary translation took a considerable amount of time, it took at least 2 to 3 months for the English version to come out, making it difficult to match the publication date with the Korean version. In fact, the timing of publication of a trend report is important, whether it is published in Korean or English. This year's preliminary translation was done in collaboration with AI, and this greatly reduced the work time, which used to take about 2 to 3 months. Professor Michel Lamblin, who was in charge of supervising the English translation, also expressed satisfaction with the AI translation. However, although AI translation is fast and has a high understanding of syntax and grammar, it is still far from able to present its results to readers "on its own," as it were. This is because our book contains a lot of new – and newly coined – words, many of which are buzzwords with subtle nuances in Korean. For example, the AI did not understand words such as "*hwa ryong jeom jeong*화룡점정,畵龍點睛," or "*buncho* society분초사회," so it came up with incorrect translations. In the end, it became evident that the human touch remains indispensable, and it may well remain so for the foreseeable future. My personal experience with AI during the publication of this book has solidified this belief. It underscores the fact that there will always be areas in which only humans can excel, and this divide may persist for quite some time in the future.

While AI can undoubtedly enhance mechanical productivity, human intervention remains crucial to meet the ever-increasing demands and expectations of consumers. In fact, it could be argued that the role of humans has become even more pivotal. This is because the distinction in quality often hinges on the unique "human touch" added at the final stages when comparing similar outcomes produced by artificial intelligence.

In a word, "*hwa ryong jeom jeong*" is necessary. This translates as "putting the finishing touches" on something, and literally refers to doing so by meticulously adding the dots on the eyes of a drawing of a dragon, symbolizing the completion of the most critical aspect of any endeavor. Even if a dragon is skillfully drawn, it lacks authenticity without those distinctive pupils in its eyes. Similarly, no matter how much AI performs a task to an approximate degree, achieving a perfect result often requires human intervention.

With this concept in mind, we chose the subtitle and main trend keyword for this book, perfectly fitting for the Year of the Dragon: DRAGON EYES. This encapsulates the idea of reaching the pinnacle of the dragon's essence, emphasizing the importance of those defining details.

Light and shadow on the Korean economy

"Will it get better next year?"

This question likely arises due to the challenging economic conditions experienced in 2023, offering a glimmer of hope for an improved economic outlook in 2024. However, the crucial question remains: Will 2024 indeed witness a tangible improvement?

In summary, the current conditions are marked by significant uncertainty. Drawing an analogy, the British economic weekly magazine *The Economist* aptly describes the post-pandemic global economy as akin to the *Mona Lisa*. Leonardo da Vinci's masterpiece is renowned for its enigmatic smile that leaves viewers uncertain whether she is smiling, sad, or wearing a frown. Similarly, the world economy's future appears just as ambiguous in the wake of the post-pandemic.

Maekyung Economy's assessment is that our economy is displaying this "Mona Lisa ambiguity," characterized by employment growth primarily in the service industry and a thriving stock market despite economic challenges. Simultaneously, there are indications of potential consumption slowdowns and real estate market vulnerabilities.

The crucial question lies in how to navigate this uncertain terrain successfully. In situations where crises and opportunities intersect, the distinction between those who gracefully leap forward and those who falter becomes increasingly evident. The ability to respond to change plays a pivotal role, and the first step in this journey is understanding the trends currently shaping our world. So, what trends will unfold in 2024?

A new trend in speedy society competing for every minute and second

The *Consumer Trend Insights* series announces ten consumer trend keywords every year and has one principle regarding the order of keyword phrases. The keyword phrases are reordered according to their first letters to complete the acronym of the year's Chinese zodiac animal, with the first keyword providing a perspective on our society for that year which thematically links and leads the rest of the keywords. The idea is to select trends that are the root cause of change. So, which keyword will take center stage in the multitude of trends expected to unfold in 2024? The answer lies in our perception of time.

"**Time-efficient society**" is the keyword that encapsulates the contemporary inclination of individuals to place immense value on the efficiency of time utilization and their relentless pursuit of maximizing the "density" of time spent. Time has transformed into a finite and invaluable resource, rivaling, if not surpassing, the significance of money in our lives. Consequently, everyone now finds themselves engaged in relentless competition for this precious commodity.

This shift isn't solely due to increased busyness but is intricately tied to the evolving economic paradigm. As we transition from an ownership-driven economy to one centered around experiences, time emerges as the paramount resource. In the realm of the experience economy, which thrives on the investment of time, it becomes instinctive to use it judiciously and seek the utmost efficiency. While money can be borrowed or earned, time remains an unrecoverable asset. Thus, the way we choose to utilize this time has assumed a position of paramount importance in our daily lives.

Shifts in thinking regarding the "cost-effectiveness of time" also influence people's actions. A notable example is the trend known as "**ditto consumption**." The word "ditto" means "me too" and represents a consumption pattern where individuals streamline their purchase decisions by following someone else's lead, content, or commerce, simply saying "me too" when buying. With product variety and distribution channels expanding along with rising quality standards, the complexities of choice and the fear of failure, often referred to as FOBO (Fear of Better Options), have grown significantly.

In a society where every minute and second holds immense value, the desire for swift, error-free choices fuels the ditto consumption phenomenon – a reflection of the need for quick decision-making in a time-conscious world.

Our ability to overcome the challenges presented by these evolving dynamics hinges on our willingness to explore unconventional possibilities through innovative efforts. In a society where the opportunity cost of time is on the rise, "**spin-off projects**" emerge as a highly effective strategy for avoiding failures. Traditionally associated with movies or dramas, "spin-offs" now extend to products, technology, businesses, and individual career development.

Particularly relevant are the "side projects" gaining popularity among office workers today. These endeavors encompass self-improvement and applications that can evolve into new career avenues – an extension of one's existing pursuits, aptly termed "career spin-offs."

Society is witnessing a growing trend toward individualization. However, as time becomes increasingly scarce for each person, the concept of "care," an essential element for human survival, takes on profound significance. The "**care economy**" signifies that the role of caregiving, once primarily undertaken by family members or directed toward socially disadvantaged individuals such as the elderly or patients, has evolved beyond simple consideration. It is now becoming a pivotal pillar of the national economy.

Rather than relying solely on oneself or one's family to fulfill this function, there is an urgent need to revamp systems and perceptions that enable technology and the community to collectively participate in caregiving. This paradigm shift within the care economy is expected to play a crucial role in addressing the challenges of a fragmented society, where ensuring the well-being of every individual has become increasingly complex.

Changes within the younger generations serve as both a consequence of and a catalyst for broader societal transformations. These individuals, born and raised in a markedly distinct economic, cultural, and technological landscape compared to their parents, foster and steer new trends with a markedly different mindset. This is precisely why our books consistently spotlight the youth.

In the current year, three "young trends" have captured considerable attention, with the most intriguing being the phenomenon known as the "**hexagonal human**." The hexagonal framework we employ for comparing and evaluating various attributes of an object is known as a "hexagonal spider graph." The hexagon is often emblematic of perfection because when all reference axes are entirely filled, it transforms into a regular hexagon.

Contemporary youth harbor admiration for "hexagonal people" – individuals who appear flawless in every conceivable facet of life, including appearance, education, wealth, occupation, family, personality, and unique skills (which may even surpass six). The hexagonal human trend can be interpreted as a form of expression that encapsulates the vigor and apprehensions of today's youth, who grapple with the societal pressure to attain an elusive state of perfection.

As the phrase "Homo ludens" implies, the desire to have fun is not a new thing, but there is a uniqueness in the fun-seeking behavior of young people these days that has never been seen before. We would like to call this behavior a facet of "**dopamine farming**" as people try to collect dopamine, the neurotransmitter secreted when we experience something new and interesting. "Farming" is a gaming term that refers to the player's act of collecting items (like harvesting crops) to improve the game character's abilities. "Dopamine farming" refers to the effort to actively try and "collect" any experience that can release dopamine, which brings pleasure. Of course, "dopamine farming" is a keyword that requires caution. This is because dopamine leads to pursuing more and more stimulating pleasures. This is why, in a busy, busy society, the balance with serotonin, which can lead to true happiness beyond short and easy fun, becomes important.

Since the home is the basic unit of consumption, even if it is a single-person household, it is always an important topic for consumer scholars. In the past, the main focus of attention was on women because housewives were the ones responsible for running the household. However, recently, a significant change has been noticed. Young husbands and fathers are taking on household management, including housework and childcare, in a completely different way than previous generations. The keyword "**millennial hubbies**" points out the causes, phenomena, and prospects of these changes. We analyzed the unprecedented appearance of today's grooms, who have not received much attention despite playing half the role of solving the low birth rate problem, which is the biggest issue Korea faces.

The ten consumer trend keywords that we announce every year can be broadly divided into two types. One is changes in the values and lifestyles of Koreans living today, and the other is institutional changes in technology, economy, and policy. If the keywords described above are about changes in people, what are the strategic trends that companies, governments, and local municipalities, etc. should pay attention to? This year, issues of prices and pricing, and of rural-urban dynamics, are becoming important.

"**Variable pricing**" is a keyword that emphasizes that prices are not fixed but can be set very dynamically, and that suppliers and distributors can set prices strategically. Now, with the advancement of data technology, it has become possible to accurately measure consumers' "willingness to pay," making it possible to vary the price of a single product or service depending on the occasion, time, and consumer product. We hope that diversified price differentiation will not just be a way to maximize the profits of producers and distributors but will also harmonize corporate growth and consumer welfare by presenting prices that consumers can understand and afford.

Recently, cities and rural regions have also been changing rapidly. Until now, this problem has been addressed with policies that cater to the increase or decrease in the residential population under the frame of polarization between large cities and local regions. However, even in large cities such as Seoul, there are areas that are marginalized, and the phenomenon of people flocking to regional towns is increasing. In a society where public transportation is developing rapidly and people's values are changing toward embracing a more nomadic lifestyle, rural areas are no longer fixed spaces – they are evolving into more fluid-like spaces. We conceptualize this trend with the term "**liquidpolitan**," in the sense that the city (polis, politan) is becoming fluid, like a liquid. We hope that in 2024, when National Assembly elections will be held to elect representatives from each regional jurisdiction, a new paradigm of regional concepts and aspirations can bring about equilibrium in Korea's regional imbalances.

The most socially and economically important keyword is "**Homo promptus**." This is a keyword about the development of artificial intelligence in the near future and the changing trends that orbit it. ChatGPT, which challenged the realm of creativity that was considered humans' unique sanctuary, was a huge shock from the moment it went mainstream. The emergence of "Generative Artificial Intelligence (GenAI)," which can churn out new creations in almost all areas such as art, writing, and coding, raises the question, "Is there anything I can do better than AI?" It raises existential issues as well. What happens next? How will trends in the market and society change? If the advent of the AI era is inevitable, how should we prepare ourselves to survive monumental change? It is important to note that "Homo" in "Homo promptus" refers to us humans, centering on what we humans should do when faced with this huge trend of progress. In order to coexist with AI and lead the era of competition, we must have both the ability to think and interpret. What is important is how to go beyond oneself toward change without being buried in the technological results of AI. Only humans with a "metacognitive" ability to reflect on themselves will be up to the task of putting the finishing touches – the *"hwa ryong jeom jeong"* – to complete the drawing of the dragon created by AI.

Readers may not notice this at the outset, but this year we have significantly changed our internal writing process, conducted our own expert interviews and focus group discussions (FGDs), and significantly increased the process of collecting internal and external feedback. The structure of the book was also reconsidered from scratch and a wide range of new alternatives were examined. As a result, the overall appearance of the book is not much different from previous years, but this continuity is the result of attempting change while keeping all possibilities open.

This is the 16th *Trend Korea* book. I try hard not to fall into inertia. Rather than being the best book, I'm trying my best to make this a better book than last year's. I sincerely hope that this book will be of greater help than last year in preparing for 2024, when readers will have to compete with recession, high prices, extreme climates, and even AI.

Fall 2023, on behalf of the authors,
Rando Kim

DRAGON EYES

CONTENTS

Don't Waste a Single Second:
Time-Efficient Society

Have you ever watched TV, flipped through a magazine, and searched for something on your smartphone all at the same time? Have you ever decided against settling down to watch a popular 16-episode drama after watching a summary video of the entire show on YouTube, so that you could still engage in water cooler talk about it? And when taking the subway, have you ever chosen the subway car closest to your next stop's transfer spot or exit?

Living a life of juggling multiple tasks has now become a daily routine. These behaviors have one thing in common: we spend our time very efficiently. Although Korean people, accustomed to "hurry, hurry culture" are always busy, the concept of time these days is significantly different from before. High importance is placed on time efficiency. It isn't just about being busy. As the economic paradigm shifts from an economy based on ownership to one based on experience, time has become as valuable a resource as money. In the past, showcasing expensive possessions was crucial, but nowadays, we're in an era where people flaunt "proofies" of their travel destinations, restaurants, or trendy places. And we watch "content" for several hours a day. All of these require a huge time investment.

With time becoming a scarce resource, we would like to name the trend of maximizing time efficiency as a feature of "*buncho* society," in which everyone lives in a constant struggle for every minute분, *bun* and second초, *cho* in their lives. In a "*buncho* society," we worship time supremacy, and in order to increase time efficiency, we (1) value "time more than money"; (2) "break down" the units of time used; (3) "juggle time" and multitask; (4) "check the conclusion first," then do the work; and (5) aim for "failure-free" shopping. The proverb "Time is money" feels more pressing than ever. Now, time has become as valuable as – or even more valuable than – money.

"9:01 is not 9:00"

This is the first principle in "11 ways to do better work" by Woowa Brothers우아한형제들, the operator of food delivery service Baedal Minjok배달의민족. It may sound like an obvious fact, but it raises an important point in our evolving conception of time. Now, breaking down usable chunks of time into one-minute units is becoming more common. "The department meeting ends at 5 o'clock, so the Zoom meeting will start at 5:17." Such minute-specific schedules are on the rise. In the past, there was a concept known as "Korean Time," where being approximately 20 to 30 minutes late was considered socially acceptable. However, in today's fast-paced world, waiting for such a duration without a specific reason has become increasingly rare. "Korean Time" has gradually faded into obscurity, and our daily lives are now meticulously managed down to the minute. This phenomenon is not exclusive to Korea but is a global trend. According to Johann Hari, the author of *Stolen Focus: Why You Can't Pay Attention*, Americans are talking more quickly, getting less sleep, and even walking about 10% faster compared to two decades ago. We are entering an era characterized by acceleration.

What about you? Do you watch TV while flipping through a magazine and searching for something on your smartphone? Do you just watch a 16-episode series' summary video on YouTube and pretend you watched it so you can make idle chit-chat with colleagues? Do you position yourself as close as possible to your next stop's transfer spot or exit on the subway, to save a few seconds?

These behaviors have one thing in common: we spend our time very efficiently. Extreme importance is placed on time efficiency and the "density" of time usage has increased significantly. Therefore, for *Consumer Trend Insights 2024*, we would like to call society's strong inclination towards maximizing time efficiency a feature of "*buncho* society." This term reflects the idea that all its members are engaged in a relentless pursuit of optimizing every minute분, *bun* and second초, *cho* of their lives.

Koreans have long been known for their fast-paced lifestyle, with the joke being that the first word foreign workers learn when they come to Korea is "*ppalli-ppalli*빨리 빨리, hurry up." However, as we enter 2024, the fact that time has emerged as a prevailing trend and is the primary focus of this book underscores the profound changes taking place. Today, time has become the most precious resource in Korean society. Let's swiftly delve into how consumers allocate their time in a society where every minute and every second holds immense value, exploring the factors contributing to the heightened significance of time and considering how industries should adapt. *Ppalli-ppalli!*

Various Aspects of *Buncho* Society

Time is more important than money

Time and money are essential resources for modern individuals. However, in the past, money was more important than time and it was natural to take the time to save money. However, these days, time and money have become equally precious, with time perhaps becoming even more precious than money. As a result, there is a growing number of people willing to spend money to gain more control over their time. This desire for efficient use of both money and time is leading to changes in various aspects of life.

"I used to spend a lot of time hunting for the lowest prices in the past because I felt satisfied when I got a great deal. Nowadays, it's too tiring, so I'd rather spend that time talking to my kids and relaxing."

- an interview with a customer by the Consumer Trend Analysis Center

For consumers, looking for the best prices has always been a common practice, both a choice and a seeming obligation. But when the value of saving time and having new experiences outweighs the value of saving money through extensive searches and price comparisons, it makes sense to forego the quest for the lowest price. Today, there are numerous activities to enjoy with the extra time one gains. This is why "time-effectiveness," which evaluates outcomes in relation to the time invested, has become just as important as cost-effectiveness, which gauges effects and performance relative to price.

With the growing emphasis on time-efficiency, people are increasingly willing to spend money on services that can save them just a little bit of time. On platforms like "Daangn Market당근마켓," where used goods are traded, unique part-time job opportunities frequently emerge as trade items. These opportunities range from helping individuals save time by walking their dogs to providing transportation for children to and from school or even waiting in line for popular local restaurants. This trend reflects a situation where the need for urgent human assistance is on the rise, coupled with an increasing demand for side hustles during one's free time.

Today, younger office workers prioritize proximity to their job more than ever before. In the past, owning a home was a top priority, leading many to buy homes in the affordable suburbs, even if it meant enduring a commute of an hour or more to work. However, now more and more people are trying to save unnecessary commuting time by reducing the distance between their residence and workplace, even if it is not their own home. In this context, an increasing number of job seekers consider the location of a company in addition to its salary, reputation, and growth potential when deciding on a job.

Breaking down units of time

"I took a 'half-half-half' day off to do some banking."

In a *buncho* society, employees meticulously modularize their work hours. Lately, more and more companies are introducing or considering the adoption of "half-half (quarter) day off" and "half-half-half (eighth) day off" options, going beyond the traditional half-day leave. This frees employees to use their allotted annual leave in units other than full or half-days, down to the hour. They use their time off flexibly according to their needs, such as doing their banking or going to the hospital. Or, they can participate in exercise programs like "Small PT짬PT," "Gap PT틈새PT," or "Semi-PT세미PT," which allow for approximately 30 to 50 minutes of exercise during lunchtime. The idea is to structure time into tightly knit modules to enhance efficiency.

Even one minute is seen as a long time now. Anyone who has experienced quickly swiping to another app when having to wait for more than a minute in a smartphone environment where content rotates by the second will sympathize. As consumer time units shorten in this way, home shopping is also changing. On the T-commerce channel CJ OnStyle Plus, they are currently running a pilot program called "Jjogaegi Show(Split Show)쪼개기쇼," where the conventional one-hour broadcasts are split down to just ten minutes.

The way we measure time shapes our thinking. The breaking down of our time units reflects a more precise and valuable use of time. Consider the traditional Korean method of breaking down time into two-hour units, starting with "Mouse hour자시子時," "Cow hour축시丑時," "Tiger hour인시寅時," etc. In a society with a slower pace of life, where agriculture was aligned with the seasons, this would have been a sufficient unit of time. With the advent of the Industrial Revolution, the economy became more industrialized and service-oriented, automobiles and railways increased the speed of transportation, and the invention of clocks improved the accuracy of time, leading people to be able to measure time in units of minutes and seconds. Salary was often called "monthly pay월급," but now asking about one's "hourly wage시급" is the more common reference point for one's income. The concept of hourly wages naturally reinforces the idea that "time is money" and makes people obsessed with saving time, even when they are not particularly busy.

Since we are all busy and don't have much time, making an appointment is not easy. It's common to see people take out their phones at every gathering, trying to coordinate the next meeting date. Accordingly, services that assist in coordinating schedules for multiple people have also emerged. The business schedule coordination service "What Time되는시간" offers a variety of options, from free services that coordinate meeting schedules between individuals to premium services for businesses that allow unlimited connections between reservation pages and calendars. When a user sends a URL for a meeting request, which is integrated with services like Naver and Google Calendar, the recipient simply needs to select available dates and times. Once done, the schedule is automatically confirmed, and the results are instantly sent to each person's email and KakaoTalk. Within just two years of its launch, the service has been experiencing continuous growth, reaching 1,400 corporate customers and 22,000 individual customers

Juggling time

"Eating, putting on makeup, playing games, sending text messages, dozing off…"

These are some of the "non-driving-related activities" drivers do when their Advanced Driver Assistance System (ADAS), also known as "semi-autonomous driving" mode, is up and running in their cars. The Insurance Institute for Highway Safety (IIHS) in the United States has revealed that 53% of Cadillac Super Cruise users and 42% of Tesla Autopilot users are misusing semi-autonomous driving modes. What do actual drivers think? Approximately half of Super Cruise users and 42% of Autopilot users consider it okay to do something else while using semi-autonomous driving mode. These days, people can't concentrate on just one thing diligently. Even though semi-autonomous vehicles issue continuous warnings and deactivate the driving mode when the driver removes their hands from the steering wheel, some people still engage in "non-driving-related activities" by purchasing auxiliary devices that trick the sensors into thinking their hands are on the wheel.

A safer example of our penchant to juggle time and multitask is audiobooks. Audiobooks are generally a medium that can be listened to while doing other things, such as driving or doing household chores, so they are an indirect indicator of how multitasking is increasing. In the smartphone realm, it has become commonplace to have multiple tabs open and perform tasks simultaneously. Smartphones also support capabilities to make it easier for users to multitask. Samsung's Galaxy Z Fold 5 introduced a "Multi-Active

Windows" function that allows users to display up to three windows on one screen. Users can perform tasks such as simultaneously viewing two browsers and sending emails, much like working at a desk with multiple monitors. In addition, the "Taskbar" function, which supports multitasking like a PC, can store up to 12 apps, including four recently used apps, in the bottom bar of the screen, allowing users to switch between apps, manage, and run them without hindering their ongoing work.

Checking the conclusion first

With the changing concept of time, the way we consume content is also changing. First, people want to know the conclusion quickly. In the past, when reviewing movies or books, the expression or hashtag "no spoilers" was frequently used to assure the taboo of spoiling a movie or series' ending or major plot point was safely avoided. However, these days, summary videos explicitly stating they contain spoilers have become more popular on YouTube. A summary video can serve as stand-alone content because it typically presents at least 80% of the plot, sometimes including the ending. Surprisingly, these summary videos have gained immense popularity and are considered as engaging as watching the original content itself. Popular binge-watching videos can sometimes achieve views comparable to the number of monthly OTT users. According to the big data analysis platform Mobile Index, the number of monthly active users (MAU) for Korean Netflix in January 2023 was 12.58 million, and the number of views of the binge-watcher's video for the Netflix original drama *The Glory* edited on a YouTube channel was 13.81 million (as of February 2023). This means that the number of people who watched the summary video was 1.2 million more than Netflix's January 2023 users.

Reflecting the desire of users to get through content more quickly, Netflix added a function in 2019 that allows viewers to choose their playback speed. Users can choose between 0.5x, 0.75x, 1x (standard), 1.25x, and 1.5x speeds, and also to quickly scrub ten seconds forward or ten seconds backward. Now we have become accustomed to watching movies by adjusting the playback speed. According to a survey conducted by LG U+'s IPTV subscribers, 39% of customers reported watching movies or dramas at a faster-than-normal speed. This means that nearly 4 out of every 10 people are viewing content at an accelerated pace, with 29% of them using the service at more than double the standard speed.

In fact, the ability to watch content quickly is largely thanks to subtitles. Subtitles allow viewers to comprehend the storyline solely by reading the dialogue, bypassing the emotional nuances of the characters and the visual aspects of the storytelling. Perhaps this is why subtitles, whether for domestic or foreign content, have been garnering renewed attention. Notably, even Korean movies are now being screened in theaters with subtitles. The Korean Film Council announced that, beginning with the release of the movie *Smugglers*밀수 in July 2023, Korean films will be shown with Korean subtitles in cinemas.

Failure-free shopping

If time is the most precious resource of all, the most regrettably squandered time is likely that spent on failure. There's nothing more disappointing than watching a 16-episode drama all the way to the end, only to be left with an unsatisfying and lackluster conclusion. Above all, the 16+ hour investment can feel like an extreme waste of time. That's why people often check the ending on YouTube first before watching the drama in earnest.

The same goes for shopping. In a world inundated with information, shopping is not just about spending money; it's also about spending significant amounts of time. Wasting money and time on unsuccessful shopping endeavors is quite a setback. Nobody wants to invest their time in a subpar product. Modern consumers, with years of online shopping experience under their belts, strive to eliminate the concept of "failed consumption." Consequently, numerous strategies are emerging to minimize these shopping mishaps. According to interviews conducted by the authors, these include intricate and detailed tidbits of know-how.

- *Refer to actual review photos from fellow buyers rather than just product images.*
- *Check the material, fabric, and finishing details directly through detailed product photos.*
- *When searching for purchase reviews, read them in order of "lowest rating" and filter out promotional "fake reviews."*
- *Do not purchase extremely cheap products.*
- *Order all sizes and colors of the same product at once, keep what fits, and return the rest to reduce the chances of failure.*

Our thinking on gifts is also changing. In the past, when a birthday came around, there was excitement and anticipation about what gift one would get. These days, things have gotten a little bit more direct. People use KakaoTalk's "Wish List" function to upload their own gift wish lists and inform their friends. According to a survey conducted by the "University Tomorrow Research Laboratory for the Twenties대학 내일 20대 연구소" in June 2022, with 900 individuals aged 15 to 41, 56.7% of the MZ generation checked their friends' wish lists, and 35.1% gave a present from the wish list. This trend is particularly pronounced among Generation Z. Among individuals in their early to mid-twenties, 66.2% check out products listed on their friends' wish lists, and 42.8% have given gifts that were on someone's wish list. Gone are the days of being surprised by unwrapping a gift. Unlike previous generations that valued the element of surprise and the unknown, today's Generation Z tends to worry about unforeseen future circumstances or unexpected situations. They lean towards minimizing effort and avoiding the risk of failure.

Therefore, "trustworthy" shopping malls become competitive. Shopping malls themselves rather than products are becoming a criterion for selection. Consumers who think, "Mall x is good for food items, Mall y for clothing, and Mall z for travel products," have their own cognitive shopping maps formed in their minds. For these consumers, services that accurately understand their preferences are even more important. The best shopping malls commonly attribute their success to AI-based "personalized product recommendation technology." AI that learns from platform purchase histories and search data, preferences displayed in products and reviews, and time spent on a specific product's page, configures the screen with only products that suit individual tastes, resulting in more purchases.

Why Has Time Become So Precious?

"Time is money" is a very old saying. Time has always been important. However, as we approach the year 2024, why has time become such an incomparably more precious resource than ever before? It's not just because our lives are busier. First, as the economic landscape shifts from an ownership-driven model to one focused on experiences, time has gained equal importance alongside money as a valuable resource. In the past, displaying expensive possessions was a priority, but today, we're in an era where people show off "proofies인증샷" of their travel destinations, dining experiences, and trendy spots – a feat made possible through investing in time. Before, we used to indulge in the weekly feature film offering from one of the main TV stations; now, with the plethora of streaming services (OTTs), we spend several hours each day consuming "content." All of these activities demand a significant amount of time. In modern society, time undeniably stands out as the most precious resource, making its preservation and efficiency a natural pursuit.

Second, IT technology that operates on a second-by-second basis also contributes to this trend. For example, in Kakao Maps you can check the ultra-precise bus routes. It utilizes satellite navigation systems to display real-time bus locations on maps, updating the bus positions by the second and allowing users to check the movement speeds based on factors like traffic signal wait times and road conditions. Given these conditions it is natural that people want to actively utilize their 24 hours by *buncho* (minute and second) increments.

Third, there's an abundance of content that demands our time for consumption. The recent surge in subscription-based content platforms such as Netflix, Millie's Library밀리의 서재, and Welaaa월라, in addition to various social media outlets like YouTube, has devoured people's time at an astonishing rate, like a black hole. We're inundated with an unprecedented volume of information. In this ceaseless sea of content, many are forsaking a regular pace of life and opting to live life at double or even triple speed. Instead of actively appreciating music, reading books, or delighting in films, we are merely passively consuming content.

Lastly, the COVID-19 pandemic has disrupted our stereotypes about time. We have experienced the forced implementation of flexible work arrangements and working from home, and the understanding that time usage can vary significantly from person to person. People have the flexibility to steer clear of congested rush hours and can opt to work during their most focused hours. As a result, individuals have diversified in terms of how they allocate their time, and the concept of standardized, uniform time has become less significant. Confronted with this trend of demassification and hyper-individualization of time, it was only natural that interest in optimizing time usage would surge. Maximizing the productivity and efficiency of everyday routines has become increasingly crucial, emphasizing the need to make the most of ordinary daily time by condensing it effectively.

Industrial Response to *Buncho* Society

Platforms scramble for time

As consumers' time becomes a critical resource in a *buncho* society, the core competitiveness of distribution now depends on how long they can retain consumers and extend their engagement time. Instagram employs various tactics to encourage millions of users to visit the app several times a day, while shopping mall apps offer various benefits to consumers to encourage them to download the apps. As the diversity of online spaces increases, time seems to pass by more quickly, which pushes these online spaces to implement various experiential elements. *Buncho* society consumers don't stay on platforms without a specific purpose, so it becomes important to keep consumers online by, for example, actively using simple but addictive games, holding instant reward events, or hosting community activities. Representative examples include "Goodoc굿닥," a hospital reservation app, "Toss토스," a financial app, and "Cash Walk캐시워크," a healthcare platform. Daangn Market also adopts gaming elements and displays user trustworthiness with their "Manner Meter매너온도" based on user praise, reviews, and bad manner penalties. The initial meter, or temperature, reading is 36.5 degrees, and it rises with positive reviews. The activity badge system is also a typical gaming element.

Offline retail stores are adjusting to the time-efficiency

trend through substantial makeovers. Shopping malls are growing in size once more, as consumers increasingly prefer to satisfy multiple shopping needs in a single location. This inclination has been amplified by the impact of the coronavirus pandemic. According to the National Association of Realtors (NAR) in the United States, although the net absorption area of general retail spaces decreased from 2017 to 2023, the net absorption area of "power centers" (shopping centers with 23,000-56,000 m^2 of gross leasable area size) expanded. This shift is attributed to the rising demand among consumers for one-stop shopping destinations where they can purchase everything they need.

The franchise industry is promptly adapting with a "relocation" store opening strategy, emphasizing the establishment of new stores within multifaceted shopping centers. As an example, the family restaurant chain Outback initiated 15 new store openings, with the majority situated in diverse shopping complexes like malls, department stores, and outlets. The results are tangible, as per Outback's reports, with the average monthly sales of the four relocated stores that opened in 2022 showing an impressive 70% increase compared to the previous year.

Reduce wait times

With changing conceptions of time, saving customers' time has become a top priority. In the service industry, it's essential to not only reduce wait times but also make sure the service is ready when the customer arrives, minimizing any unnecessary gaps. For instance, "remote queueing services" help users visit a restaurant at their reservation time without having to wait in line at the front. During the pandemic, this service was expanded to comply with social distancing measures. Even after the pandemic's end, it continues to be favorable among consumers who value their time. According to "NHN data," a domestic data analysis platform, the number of restaurant reservation app installations increased significantly in the second half of 2022 compared to the first half of 2022. "Catch Table캐치테이블" showed a 65% increase, and "Tabling테이블링" showed a 44% increase.

Smart waiting services that were primarily operated in the dining industry are now expanding into various other industries. When "Big Hit Music" launched the BTS pop-up store "BTS Pop-Up: House of BTS," they also introduced a waiting service called "Now Waiting" using KakaoTalk. This service allowed fans waiting to enter the store to spend their free time not standing in line. Fans could register their contact information and wait comfortably in the waiting service area near the pop-up store. Once they received an entry notification message, approximately 150 people could gather and enter the store as a group. Thanks to this waiting service, fans were spared from waiting in line for a combined total of roughly 10.92 million minutes, equivalent to about

182,000 hours. Each customer who utilized this service could spend their approximately 136-minute wait time away from lines.

Outlook and Implications

Buncho Society's New Business Models

What should be considered when applying this new concept of time efficiency to business models?

First, pioneer new businesses by finding customers' "gap time." It's possible to create new products or services and adjust their prices based on how different times are valued. For example, until 2006, McDonald's in Korea only opened at lunch, targeting lunch and dinner customers. What about breakfast? McDonald's looked for gap time based on consumers and developed the breakfast set "McMorning," which was a huge success. When exploring opportunities for innovative products and services in saturated markets, consumers' gap time can provide a fresh perspective.

Second, the unit of timeliness must be reduced to the level of minutes and seconds. Products and services that immediately meet consumer needs are called "On-Demand," with this immediacy being a crucial factor. Consumers prefer to secure the time and products or services they want when their needs arise. To do so, it's necessary to observe consumer behavior minute by minute and capture the moments when those needs arise. The iPhone's camera is a representative example. If it's suddenly difficult to operate the camera at the moment you want to take a picture, you might miss that moment. So, Apple improved the ease of taking photos. Even without entering a password on the lock screen, they made it possible to take photos right away by simply swiping the camera icon up or to the side on the home screen. There's not a moment to waste – or a photo to miss – in a *buncho* society.

Third, what is more important than fast service is the promise of punctuality. In a time-efficient *buncho* society, informing consumers about the exact delivery time of products or services has become a basic requirement. Even if you wait for the same amount of time, the feeling is very different at a bus stop that informs you how many minutes until your bus arrives compared to a stop that does not. This is why apps like Baedal Minjok or KakaoT also provide estimated arrival times down to the minute and second. For today's consumers who prefer managing their time and living more systematically, it's crucial to precisely inform them about the start and end times of services.

Nevertheless, we need space

Leading a busy life can indeed bring satisfaction, along with a sense of pride, in being productive and proactive. However, it's essential to consider some important factors. The vast increase in the amount of exposed and rapidly flowing information comes at a cost. Johann Hari, author of *Stolen Focus*, diagnosed that we are sacrificing "depth" in every dimension. As the title of the book suggests, we are losing our capacity of concentration. In a situation where we have to keep abreast of everything and constantly send emails, we have no time for depth. Hari warns that everything requiring depth is being weakened. It means we are unable to dive deep and we are instead increasingly just floating on the surface.

How long do people typically spend in front of artworks at the Tate Gallery in London? Surprisingly, it's only eight seconds. That's the amount of precious time we allocate for appreciating each artwork during a gallery visit. In fact, eight seconds is also the average attention span in many aspects of our lives today. Whether it's reading an article, listening to music, watching a movie, or engaging in conversation, once those eight seconds pass, our focus tends to wane. It's even shorter than the attention span of a goldfish! The attention span of Homo sapiens, the species that prides itself for conquering the Earth, has declined to a level worse than that of a goldfish. This is the price we pay for our hectic lives, where we constantly compete for every available minute and second. Undoubtedly, smartphones play a significant role in this decline. According to a study by Microsoft Canada, our attention span, which was 12 seconds in 2000 before the advent of smartphones, has dwindled to just two-third of that in a few short years. So, by 2023, it's likely much shorter than eight seconds.

Have you ever attempted a quick check of your socials, only to find yourself unable to put down your smartphone for a whole hour? This is the price we pay for constantly juggling our time. Continuous swiping and switching erodes our concentration. This phenomenon, known as the "switch cost effect," also applies to our brains. When we switch from one task to another, our brains need to reset. They have to recall what we were previously engaged in and what we were thinking, and this takes a bit of time. According to a study conducted by Michigan State University in 2015 on hospital emergency situations, continuous interruptions in the emergency room resulted in 208 errors out of 239 prescriptions. When doctors were interrupted, the error rate increased by 282%, and multitasking during work led to a 186% increase in errors.

We always need to remember what we are losing amidst the benefits of *ppalli ppalli* in a *buncho* society. Especially for us members of "Homo promptus," living with generative AI, cultivating our analog capabilities for contemplation and self-reflection becomes increasingly vital. This skill is honed when we embrace the virtues of pausing and patiently waiting. It's crucial to create room for our thoughts to wander, separate from the overwhelming speed, constant transitions and interruptions, and intense stimuli of our fast-paced world. We require blank moments of space to nurture this capability.

Rise of
'Homo Promptus'

Hello! How can I help you?

Let me ask you ...

We've all been astounded by the rise of "generative AI," capable of creating new works in various domains, including writing, coding, art, and even PowerPoint presentations. The emergence of ChatGPT, which can write lyrics and compose music, prompts an existential question: "Is there anything I can do better than AI?" What does the future hold, and how will market and societal trends evolve in the face of the inevitable AI era? What should we prepare for, and how can we thrive in this new landscape?

We seek to address these inquiries through the concept of "Homo promptus." "Promptus" refers to the medium and approach for interacting with AI and the overarching strategy for leveraging generative AI effectively. Homo promptus is the new type of human who adeptly engages with AI services, engaging in rapid, ping-pong-like exchanges with various AIs to enhance their own unique human creativity.

AI's advantages are expected to materialize in "vertical services," seamlessly integrated into various existing applications across different sectors, like retail, travel, and finance. AI will enhance existing services and significantly boost daily productivity. However, there is a growing concern that AI will lead to the reduction of simple, repetitive jobs, potentially exacerbating disparities among countries and social classes.

While entrepreneurs leading disruptive innovations required a bold spirit and decisive action, "AI-preneurs," who maximize achievements by freely utilizing AI, ironically need to cultivate humanistic critical skills. Analogous human abilities become increasingly crucial. It is imperative not to become fixated on the technical outcomes of AI but to focus on how we can drive personal transformation. Those capable of "metacognition," the ability to introspect, will be qualified to put the finishing touches on the pictures drawn by AI.

Daniel Radcliffe held up a picket sign. Tom Cruise and Margot Robbie also joined strikes boycotting promotional events for movies. Many Hollywood stars, including Meryl Streep, George Clooney, and Leonardo DiCaprio, are donating large sums of money to fellow unknown actors who are on strike. The main cause of the strikes is artificial intelligence. In May of 2023, the Writers Guild of America launched a strike, with SAG-AFTRA (the Screen Actors Guild – American Federation of Television and Radio Artists) soon following suit in July. It was the first time since 1960 that the two unions held a joint strike, and the main trigger was the threat to survival caused by generative AI. The Writers Guild of America argues that AI should not be used to write or rewrite scripts, or to serve as source material. Actors are also vehemently opposed to the proposal of having digitally captured faces of background actors used and replicated indefinitely by AI for just one day's wages.

This is a scene that clearly shows how much the development of AI will impact the creative realm, which was considered a sanctuary for humans only. This incident is noteworthy in that it received backlash from writers and actors. While there have always been concerns that the emergence of new technologies, such as the steam engine or computer, threatens human jobs, the belief that humans' one and only sanctuary – the creative realm – is populated by writers and actors, has endured.

The emergence of generative AI, which produces new creations through comparative learning with existing data, came as a great shock to many of us. Until now, we have firmly believed that the realm of creation is the last bastion of pure human activity and endeavor. However, we are currently witnessing many generative AIs performing creative acts in almost all areas, such as journalism, art, literature, development projects, and design, and including creative acts such as writing lyrics, composing music, writing articles, and drawing pictures.

The concerns of Hollywood actors are also backed up by the statistics. In May 2023, "artificial intelligence" was added for the first time as a reason behind employee layoffs as compiled in data by one firm in the United States. Challenger, Gray & Christmas (CG&C), the American outplacement firm, announced that American companies plan to reduce their combined workforce by 80,089 in 2023, citing various reasons for layoffs, of which 3,900 were "due to AI."

What happens next? What can humans do now? Will my job disappear? How will trends in the market and society change? If the AI era is inevitable, how can we utilize it effectively? How on earth should we prepare ourselves, and what can we do to survive?

In *Consumer Trend Insights 2024*, we would like to answer these questions through the keyword "Homo promptus." "Promptus" is just Latin for "prompt," as in the command prompt that awaits inputs from a person to tell a computer what to do. Anyone who used a computer with MS-DOS before Windows will remember the "C:\>_" (or C:₩>_ in Korea) prompt on the screen. The flashing underscore where you enter commands is called a prompt. To put it simply, a prompt is a channel and method of communicating with software (increasingly of the AI variety) and is a ping-pong way of exchanging questions and answers with AI.

The most important thing in making good use of generative AI services is to ask questions well. Even if one is working with the same content, the level of results varies greatly depending on how the questions are asked. Therefore, "prompt engineering" has also developed as a field that specializes in asking questions elaborately and interacting efficiently with AI. Prompt engineers are also called "AI trainers" or "AI whisperers," and they are not jobs given only to data scientists or experts with a considerable understanding of machine learning; now that anyone can communicate with AI using prompts, all people who use generative AI are directly or indirectly doing prompt engineering.

There is a saying, "AI can only be as smart as the prompt." This is because how the prompt was written determines the quality of the answer generated by AI. The operating principles of AIs that are currently attracting attention, such as OpenAI's ChatGPT, Google's Bard, and Microsoft's Bing, are all based on language models which learn hundreds of billions of words and then provide answers based on the learned data. Essentially, it is prediction. Here, the data exploration power for prediction varies depending on the user's question, or prompt, and the quality of answers provided also varies greatly.

Prompt engineering, then, is not just about how to ask questions, but also about the overall direction of how to use generative AI. Accordingly, *Consumer Trend Insights 2024* proposes "Homo promptus" as a new type of human who can lead the era of artificial intelligence through harmonious interaction with it. "Homo promptus" refers to a person who can efficiently use AI services at the right time and place to further enhance human creativity.

Whenever a new technology appears, understanding and literacy are needed, and Homo promptus is no exception. The necessary literacy is not just about how to use AI. As will be described later, it includes literacy skills from the humanities that aid in utilizing generative AI while creatively supplementing the shortcomings of AI. In that sense, it is worth noting that this keyword starts with "Homo," which means "human." At a time when new generative AI-related technologies and services emerge day by day, it means not just chasing technological changes, but thinking about what we humans should do amidst this mega-trend of great progress.

Near Future of AI: Direction of Social and Economic Development

In order to discuss how we, as Homo promptus, will cope with the coming era of artificial intelligence, it is necessary to first look at the direction of the near-future development of generative AI in terms of society and the economy. What needs to be emphasized first here is that the outlook should be on society and the economy rather than AI technology. Of course, it is necessary to understand the direction of technological developments, but what is really important are the social and economic implications of how such technology will be applied to businesses and how it will change the market. Second, we would like to limit the scope of the direction of change to the near future, about three years or so, rather than the distant future. This is because AI technology has only recently penetrated society, and the speed of its development is dizzyingly fast.

When talking about the advent of an AI society, the most

curious among us ask whether artificial intelligence that thinks at a human level can emerge, and if so, when? Many people seem to vaguely fear this the most. This level of artificial intelligence is called "AGI (artificial general intelligence)," and like Jarvis from the *Iron Man* movies or Hal 9000 from *2001: A Space Odyssey*, it can learn, judge, and create in any given situation. Experts predict that there is a 50% chance that human-level generative AI will appear before 2061, and a 90% chance that it will appear within the next 100 years.

Unlike other technologies, many people are afraid of AI due to the concern that technology will someday overwhelm humans. Even if you don't imagine AI starting a war or attempting to annihilate humans as we've seen in sci-fi movies, the vague fear of "Won't the majority of humans eventually be replaced by machines?" and "Isn't the intrinsic value of humanity disappearing?" seems to be greater than ever. The emergence of generative AI raises the existential question: "Is there anything I can do better than AI now?"

But whether we're afraid or not, new technology wets the world just as rainwater wets the ground. There is a need for regulation on some AI technologies, but it only temporarily delays the momentum. What we need to do now is to anticipate how AI technology will proceed in the near future and set the stage for social, organizational, and personal countermeasures that we, Homo promptus, can utilize.

So, what impact will generative AI have on the economy

in the near future, especially in 2024? After the advent of ChatGPT, many people accessed the site and entered the command "Do XXX" and were equally surprised and disappointed with the results. However, the value of AI services is expected to be demonstrated in so-called "vertical services," which combine various existing services and applications used in different sectors. In other words, it is to upgrade existing services by utilizing AI in various areas such as distribution, travel, and finance.

OpenAI introduced the generalized ChatGPT service to the public while also disclosing its API. "API" (application programming interface) refers to a collection of functions that allow developers in each field to easily use the functions in their services or apps. The fact that OpenAI has released its API means that the ChatGPT function can now be used across all services and platforms. ChatGPT plugins are services that connect specific software or websites to ChatGPT and allow users to search for information using data supplied through it. They are plugins in the sense that they provide additional functions, like plugs that can be inserted and removed from an outlet or motherboard. They allow consumers to easily use additional functions within their web browser of choice.

As of July 2023, there are 823 companies using ChatGPT plugins, receiving important help in innovating the service industry through work automation, increased efficiency, and improved customer experience.

In summary, the various services previously provided will, through the use of generative AI, become more convenient. In other words, even if we do not directly access services such as ChatGPT or Bard, we will be using AI services without realizing it when we use apps on our computers or smartphones. Even at this moment, new business models applying AI are being introduced.

What Do We Need?

Computer language replaced by everyday language

An important reason for the explosive public interest in and social impact of AI services is their ease of use. Andrej Karpathy, an AI expert formerly head of Tesla's AI and now working at OpenAI, said on X (formerly Twitter) that "the hottest new programming language is English." "English" here should not be understood as the specific language of English itself but rather as all "living languages" that we use daily. In other words, computer language is being replaced by human language. Now, it is possible to use computers to perform knowledge work or creative activities using only everyday language, even if one does not know a particular computer language. Another reason why ChatGPT had a large ripple effect is because it used the very simple and familiar communication method of chatting. Chatting is a familiar practice that has always accompanied PC communication. The very natural act of chatting, and the prompt that elicits an input in natural language, is a key factor that has allowed ChatGPT to become a game changer in the artificial intelligence world.

Furthermore, AI that can communicate with various senses beyond natural language is expected to emerge in the near future. AI will have eyes and ears, and we will be able to talk to it in various ways by adopting various types of languages. ChatGPT released GPT-4 in March 2023, which is already equipped with a "multi-modal" function that allows users to acquire information in various ways other than visual, auditory, and via text. Generative AI's sensory communication function will be developed further, and human simulation capabilities will become much more advanced.

Not AI, but prompts

As AI becomes easy enough for the average person to use, prompt engineering and prompt engineers will become more important. In fact, with the recent increase in the preference for prompt engineers, companies that promise a huge annual salary of 400 million won have begun to emerge overseas. Anthropic, an AI startup founded by senior members of OpenAI, posted a job posting for prompt engineers and data library managers with an annual salary of

$250,000-$375,000 USD.

In the digital art category of the Colorado State Fair Art Competition in August 2022, the winning painting became a hot topic; it had been drawn with generative AI program Midjourney. Moreover, Jason Allen, who submitted the painting, received even more attention when it was revealed he wasn't a painter but a game designer. He is said to have completed the winning work, *Théâtre d'Opéra Spatial*스페이스 오페라극장, after entering over 900 prompts. So, who owns the copyright to this image? Allen asked the U.S. Copyright Office to recognize the copyright to the painting. But despite the seemingly artistic merit of a first prize winning painting, the request was rejected. A federal U.S. district court also ruled "denial of copyright application" in a lawsuit filed by an inventor seeking recognition of copyright for artwork they created with AI.

The legal principle of the U.S. Copyright Office and courts is that copyright cannot be recognized for works "without any creative input or intervention from a human author." Moreover, generative AI is not considered pure creation because it produces results by learning from data that already exists and that has been created by humans. But in terms of prompts, it's a slightly different story. Some prompt engineers are even selling their own prompts.

It is common to sell and purchase computer commands in markets such as PromptBase. Since 2021, more than

25,000 people have traded prompts, and as of February 2023, 700 prompt engineers are selling e-book prompts. Allen, who created *Théâtre d'Opéra Spatial*, also refused to disclose the prompts he entered until the final result was obtained. The logic is that although the painting itself is not a person's creation, the process leading to the result is one's own creation.

If you have to give over 900 prompts to draw a picture, some people might think, "I'd rather draw it myself." But this is the key: Allen, not AI, created the picture based on his prompts. Metaphorically speaking, if AI is a canvas, the prompts are the paint and brushes. The emphasis of the creative process is on the prompt, not on AI. Even if we do not aim to become prompt engineers, an understanding of prompts is essential if we are to navigate as Homo promptus through these turbulent times of the new AI.

So, what are the capabilities that Homo promptus must have? To answer this question, reflection on "human things" is needed again. What a prompt engineer needs is experience using generative AI and logical and verbal conversation skills, rather than coding skills. In addition to knowledge of basic programming languages and machine learning, a humanistic understanding of history, philosophy, law, and linguistics is also necessary. Furthermore, considering the increasingly segmented nature of AI services, it is necessary to also have professional knowledge in relevant fields such as public affairs, finance, distribution, medicine, law, and manufacturing.

It is often said that "what is easy for humans is difficult for computers, and what is difficult for humans is easy for computers," which is essentially what is known as Moravec's Paradox. In other words, if computers and humans can properly combine their powers, they can achieve great results. Therefore, in order to lead in the era of AI, it is necessary to focus human capabilities on areas in which AI has no foothold.

Which human capabilities are difficult to find in AI? When you ask AI various questions and then read the answers, you often get the feeling that "yes, this seems plausible, but something is lacking." So, you fill in the gaps by repeating the question, but there are still subtleties and small variables that need to be continually fine-tuned. And that's just it: Homo promptus, the human capacity to lead the era of AI, depends on those subtleties. For example, it is said that when AI is used in work, it is possible to obtain results equivalent to 70-80% of existing results with only 20% of the usual effort. In the end, Homo promptus' capabilities depend on using the remaining 80% of effort to fill in the 20-30% of missing subtleties that AI has difficulty with.

In the same context, it is worth paying attention to the argument and its logic that AI will not completely replace one of the internet's most powerful tools: search. If existing leading search engines are equipped with AI, will the current way we search for information disappear completely? Unlike existing search engines that provide answers by showing multiple links, AI presents the desired answer directly without links. The advantage is that it can greatly reduce the "depth" – the stcps users must take – through which users obtain information.

However, in the process of finding an answer, rather than leaving it entirely to AI by asking numerous questions, users sometimes opt to access the information they want by looking at the results listed by search and clicking on the link that interests them. It is said that the answer "depth" of AI is reduced, but this depends on the number of questions required to obtain the desired answer. There is a high probability that users will choose to use search and AI according to the situation at the time.

This is not just a question for search but is also related to the answer to how AI will be used by consumers in the future. It is highly likely that AI will be used as a powerful assistant that can help distinguish between areas that need help from AI and areas that do not.

It's up to humans

This is perhaps natural. The operating principle of AI is to learn from a huge amount of existing data and then construct the most likely answer to a question. Therefore, content outside the scope of existing data cannot be learned through machine learning and cannot be answered. Instead, we get errors called "hallucinations."

The hallucination problem is expected to gradually improve through the use of synthetic data, but the important fact is that human judgment still plays an important role in the outcomes of AI. AI cannot self-evaluate how good or bad its results are. In other words, the final judgment and choice is ultimately up to humans.

In the end, the judgment on the results of AI depends on the ability to think critically. So, how can we develop this capability? Pulitzer Prize-winning author George Anders suggests that so-called "useless" liberal arts can cultivate this ability. We have the creativity to control AI by enriching the seemingly useless humanities knowledge, that is, the intellectual ability to explore the essence of humans and society. Although AI is said to be challenging the realm of creativity unique to humans, the evolving creativity that produces new structures and frameworks still remains within the human realm. The true Homo promptus is a talented individual who can freely use AI by developing this area. If the spirit of challenge and action were essential for the entrepreneur, who led destructive innovation, the "AI-preneur" who freely utilizes AI to maximal effect needs humanistic critical thinking skills. The most human analog capabilities become of the utmost importance.

Outlook and Implications

Coexistence of optimism and pessimism

New technologies have always caused conflict. The Luddite movement in 19th-century England was radical in that workers who feared the loss of their jobs to newly invented weaving machines went out to destroy those machines. This is an example of extreme technophobia. There is also an opposing, more optimistic view. Until now, there have been concerns that jobs will disappear whenever new technologies such as computers, the internet, and smartphones appear, but the view is that the number of new jobs needed in related industries is greater, ultimately increasing jobs and improving human welfare.

Of course, the answer would lie somewhere in the middle between these two extreme views, but which side would AI lean closer to? The argument that "this time is different – jobs will really disappear" and the argument that "technology has always created more new jobs" conflict with one another.

To put it bluntly, the discussion seems to lean somewhat toward pessimism. In May 2023, the World Economic Forum predicted that 69 million new jobs will be created worldwide over the next five years, but 83 million will disappear. Goldman Sachs' outlook is even bleaker. It is believed that 69% of all jobs are exposed to the impact of AI and up to 50% can be replaced by AI, so about 300 million full-time jobs worldwide could become automated.

Moreover, even if rooted in optimism, the reorganization of jobs by AI will accelerate unbalanced structural changes and further widen the gaps between countries, classes, and talent. Although jobs will increase in some advanced countries with strong AI competitiveness, the situation in middle-income and developing countries with many simple, repetitive jobs will worsen significantly. This is true even within a country. The gap between those who have Homo promptus capabilities and those who do not will widen further.

So what preparations are needed to respond to these changes?

'Responsible AI' for a new social system

As the impact of change is large, voices for "responsible AI" are loud. Following the "Digital Divide," which is still a social problem, the "AI Divide" will also widen, and as mentioned above, concerns about jobs, copyright, and personal information protection are also emerging as major issues. The European Union has been working on a draft bill to regulate AI starting in 2021 and passed a negotiated bill to introduce the world's first AI technology regulation law in June 2023. According to this law, companies operating generative AI are required to disclose the copyright of raw data used for learning. If negotiations on the bill are concluded in 2023, it is expected that the regulations will be applied starting in 2026. In Korea, the Ministry of Science and ICT과학기술정보통신부 announced in May 2023 that it will support the enactment of the "Artificial Intelligence Framework Act" to foster growth in the AI industry and create a foundation of trust. Then, in July, the Ministry of Economy and Finance기획재정부 announced its intention to revise the Copyright Act to establish new requirements and grounds for exemption from copyright infringement when using data for AI learning purposes. In the end, the key is how to nurture a growing industry while mitigating social and economic shock amid the conflict between AI and existing social systems.

A more fundamental response to the need for a new social system suited to the era of AI is also being discussed. World-renowned historian Yuval Harari also advocated the idea that instead of humans being kicked out of their jobs, robots and AI can do the work, pay taxes, and then humans receive a basic income through those taxes. Going further, Sam Altman, the founder of Open AI, also announced "Worldcoin (WLD)" for universal basic income. He announced that he would pay Worldcoin, a cryptocurrency, as a universal basic income to anyone who agrees to iris recognition, and over 1.8 million people around the world have already since been issued "World IDs." As the creator of ChatGPT, his argument is that he will provide social support for job losses resulting from the development of AI and then redistribute the value it creates. But the counterarguments are also formidable. Some criticize this, saying that this is groundwork to create an entirely different business model by collecting iris information from all of humankind.

Whether the price of iris information corresponds to the value of one Worldcoin, and whether there is a huge conspiracy or not, is actually outside the core of the universal basic income system. The reality of the universal basic income system is that it is an extremely market-oriented idea rather than a redistribution policy. Due to new technologies such as computers, the internet, smartphones, and AI, the wealth gap will grow incomparably compared to the past, so the goal is to maintain consumers with purchasing power by distributing the minimum universal basic income. Perhaps the fact that a leader of an AI business is calling for a universal basic income system gives us an idea as to how wide the wealth gap will be in the future.

Active responses are also needed from various organizations, including schools, private companies, and public institutions. Particularly for companies, whether or not they have their own data, the competitiveness of their main services, the diversity of their product portfolio, and resolving risk factors such as copyright issues will be factors that determine future success or failure.

Agility is key

Recently, Korean companies have also been entering the fray of generative AI. For example, Hyundai Department Store is trying out various advertising copies by introducing "Lewis," an AI copywriting system. Using Naver's HyperCLOVA X as its basic engine, Lewis creates new advertising text by intensively learning about 10,000 pieces of data that received a positive response from consumers among the advertising copy and phrases used at promotional events at their department stores over the past three years. Lewis says he can come up with different messages for each target. If the "art fair" target, say, is set to people in their 20s, a phrase would be put out, like: "Wanna be an insider인싸 (a popular Korean slang word that also means a person who responds quickly to trends and gets along well with many people; *inssa*) Then come to Hyundai." Or if the target is set to people in their 50s, the phrase would be: "We invite you to a department store – where art flows."

There are concerns, however, that AI advertising may produce visual material and text that is offensive and inaccurate to the public. For this reason, the phenomenon of "AI indecision," where one cannot decide whether to use AI results or not, is often observed. It is also worth noting that some companies are banning the use of generative AI due to security risks. To receive help from AI, you must first provide information, but how much risk you can take with this has emerged as a sensitive issue.

The key to utilizing AI lies in agility, not completeness. In other words, it is important that the time taken so far can be dramatically reduced. In the case of Hyundai Department Store, as a result of testing Lewis, it was said that copywriting, which normally takes about two weeks, was reduced to an average of three to four hours. In this way, generative AI is expected to bring about a revolution in speed that will dramatically shorten existing work hours. Today, time and speed have become important resources that are difficult to compare with anything else, and the introduction of generative AI appears to be an essential choice to save time and costs.

As seen in several cases, large corporations with strong financial resources are currently active in using generative AI, while relatively small organizations or self-employers do not seem to have dared to do so. However, the emergence of Homo promptus signals the popularization and democratization of AI technology. With the help of AI, you can improve productivity in daily tasks using word processors, spreadsheet or slide presentation software, and you can easily process unstructured and unorganized data, too. Opportunities are opening up for even small organizations to utilize generative AI services.

Just as it has become impossible to live without a smartphone, we are now witnessing a world where it will become difficult to live without the benefits of AI. Accordingly, changes in consumption methods and consumption forces, as well as changes in the consumption ecosystem and topography, are expected to accelerate. Just as coding has recently become a core subject, in the near future, where prompt engineering becomes commonplace, the capabilities of an AI-preneur with the ability to understand and utilize the AI ecosystem and systematically communicate with AI will become necessary.

In his book *AI Big Bang*, Professor Kim Jae-in김재인 of Kyung Hee University quotes Nietzsche in saying that humans can be more human when they "go beyond." The German philosopher emphasized that humans are beings who transcend and go beyond themselves through the concept of the *Übermensch*. Humans are beings who do not stay in the zone of averageness and mediocrity but go outward and beyond to add new and creative content.

The answer is right here. Rather than being immersed in the technological results of AI, it is important to reflect on oneself and go beyond oneself toward change. Earlier, we pointed out that AI cannot self-evaluate whether the results it produces are good or bad. The ability to reflect on oneself is called "metacognition," and only introspective humans have it. In the end, only humans who can reflect on themselves will be qualified to put the finishing touches on AI's creations – *hwa ryong jeong jeom*화룡점정 that dots the eyes of the dragon drawn by AI.

Aspiring to Be
a Hexagonal Human

"So-and-so, a 'hexagonal' celebrity, possesses it all: looks, fashion sense, athleticism, and personality." But what does "hexagonal" mean? It refers to a "hexagonal spider graph," symbolizing perfection when all axes are full. Nowadays, especially among the youth, the pursuit of perfection spans appearance, education, wealth, career, family, personality, and talents, to name a few. These individuals are known as "hexagonal humans." In their quest to become their ideal selves, they engage in activities such as:

(1) Wall-building: setting high standards that distinguish themselves from others (but also are difficult, making "hexagonalism" a difficult goal.)

(2) Quantification: measuring everything in monetary or numerical terms to prove their "hexagonality."

(3) Hexagonal play: light-heartedly caricaturing the challenging journey of achieving this hexagonal status.

Today's youth prefer "complete idols" who are flawless from the start, connecting with them to fulfill their fantasy of being treated in the same way. This "hexagonal syndrome" is largely driven by social media, as comparisons with peers globally create intangible and tangible pressures. What used to be one-dimensional competition, like academic prowess, has evolved into a complex struggle over appearance appearance, fashion, talents, and family background. The "hexagonal human" trend could be a fantastical pursuit of living in an almost "godly갓생, god+life" way, or it could be a reflection of hierarchy issues in modern Korean society. Regardless, it reflects the vitality and despair of young people under immense social pressure to be perfect.

*"I will reveal the real past of Eun Mi-hwa. The 'golden spoon' and 'golden girl*엄친딸*' stories are all nonsense. During high school, she was practically invisible. Her father worked in the meat processing industry? In the Fourth Industrial Revolution era, is a butcher even considered part of the livestock industry? Haha!"*

- From the Netflix Drama, Celebrity

In the first half of 2023, a popular drama titled *Celebrity* aired on Netflix, featuring a memorable scene. In this scene, the protagonist, Seo Ari, encounters her childhood friend Oh Min-hye, who has become a renowned fashion entrepreneur with annual revenues in the tens of billions of won, making her the top celebrity on social media. However, Min-hye strangely conceals the fact that she grew up in an ordinary middle-class family and packages her childhood as if she were the daughter of a wealthy family. As fate would have it, she coincidentally meets the protagonist, leading to the revelation of her true upbringing and the ensuing difficulties she faces in the public eye.

Doesn't something seem odd here? The notion of coming from a middle-class family as being something to hide reflects the changing discourse on "celebrity" in society today. In the past, people preferred narratives of human triumph, starting with nothing but their bare hands and grit, and overcoming difficult family backgrounds to achieve success. So, shouldn't Oh Min-hye have taken pride in her ordinary family background instead of fearing the revelation of this fact?

#HexagonCelebrities, #HexagonIdols, #HexagonWomen, #HexagonMen, #HexagonBrands, #HexagonAthletes, #HexagonMidfielders... Recently, the hashtag #Hexagon has prefixed popular social media search terms. In July 2023, when Ahn Yujin, a member of the girl group IVE, made her ceremonial appearance at a soccer stadium in Daejeon, the in-stadium announcer introduced her as "Ahn Yujin, the hexagonal entertainer who excels in singing, dance, looks, artistic talent, leadership, and even loves soccer, begging the question, 'What can't she do?'" When introducing someone to potential dating partners, you might also hear phrases like, "Mr./Ms. so-and-so is a hexagonal man/woman with exceptional looks, fashion sense, athletic ability, personality, and more." There's even a recently published book titled *Hexagon Developer*육각형 개발자 that suggests a true developer needs to excel not only in coding and basic IT skills but also in leadership and communication through writing. It seems like the term "hexagon" is being naturally used in nearly every profession.

When comparing and analyzing various attributes of a subject, people often draw a hexagonal image with criteria as axes, which is referred to as a "hexagonal spider graph." In this graph, when all the criteria axes are fully filled, it forms a perfect hexagon, symbolizing perfection, and that's why the term "hexagon" is often used to signify perfection. Nowadays, especially among individuals in their 20s and 30s, there is a fervid pursuit of this hexagonal perfection.

For example, if someone is a singer, it's not just about having a good singing voice but also being well-mannered, coming from a well-off family, and showing signs of being nurtured with love. For those who are wealthy, it's not enough to have money; they need to create wealth while contributing to personal development, earning the envy of others. We refer to people who aspire to be perfect in all aspects, including appearance, education, assets, career, family background, personality, talents, and more (which can be more than six), as "hexagonal humans."

The trend of becoming a hexagonal human manifests in several interesting ways. Firstly, hexagonal individuals set stringent standards that not everyone can achieve, asserting that it's not something anyone can become and attempting a kind of "wall-building." They prioritize elements that are seemingly destined rather than achievable through effort.

Nowadays, popular webtoons and dramas among the younger generations do not favor the narrative of "success by dint of hard work." Instead, they feature protagonists who are perfect right from the start. Secondly, they "quantify" how close they are to being hexagonal and use numbers to measure their worth, comparing and ranking themselves accordingly. They meticulously categorize factors like the prestige of their alma mater, place of residence, or job, and constantly evaluate and size themselves up against one another. Lastly, they approach the pursuit of becoming a hexagonal human with a playful attitude. They enjoy it like a game, making light of the unattainable ideal through what's called the "hexagonal game."

The trend of becoming a hexagonal human is two-sided and contentious. While younger generations may readily identify with it, older generations might scratch their heads in confusion. Furthermore, it can be considered more of a sub-trend observed among some rather than a mega-trend that all young people follow. It has both positive aspects, such as instilling a passion for pursuing one's perfect self, and negative aspects, as it can lead to despair in the pursuit of unattainable perfection that can't be achieved through effort alone. Perhaps it could be just the tip of the larger iceberg, showcasing the social issue of class stratification in modern Korean society.

Currently, South Korea's twenty to thirty-somethings

are said to be the luckiest generation, born with the highest income and educational levels since the founding of the nation. However, humans are inherently comparative beings. In an era where economic growth has slowed, and opportunities are dwindling, they live in a time where they can engage in comparisons of everyone against everyone through various social media platforms. The weight of life for young people who must engage in endless competition with anonymous others, who may scrutinize them at anytime, anywhere, is heavier than ever before. The trend of striving for a hexagonal self through constant comparison with perfect individuals – or at least those who appear perfectly hexagonal – is both an expression of vitality and despair for some young individuals who must endure this pressure. However, it's also a form of play in this challenging landscape.

People Who Aspire to Be Hexagonal Humans

1. Building walls: Not just anyone can be hexagonal

There's a recurring conversation pattern on platforms like "Blind," where many professionals anonymously share their candid stories. When someone posts online, "I finally crossed the 6 million won monthly salary mark," the comments aren't filled with the usual congratulatory "well done." Instead, they inquire about whether the person owns a house, how much they've saved, or if they have monthly expenses for their parents. When someone confesses to being a doctor, rather than receiving praise, there are more comments asking if they come from a wealthy family, if they are tall, or if they have average looks. It's not enough to have a high-income stable profession; you have to be perfect in various ways.

In the United States, the expression "effortlessly perfect" gained popularity. Originating at Duke University in 2003, this term referred to the obsession of students, especially females, who wanted to appear as if they effortlessly excelled in academics, had a great physique, were beautiful, smart, and popular without seeming to put in any effort.

A similar phenomenon can be observed in South Korea today. People here admire those who appear perfect without visibly exerting much effort and recognize them as "hexagonal individuals." Pursuing perfection in all aspects, including appearance, education, assets, career, family background, personality, and talents, represents a form of "wall-building." Achieving a good job or a high salary through effort alone is no longer a sufficient condition to be considered a hexagonal individual. To earn that recognition, one must be perfect even in areas that are not easily attainable, perhaps even those that seem destined.

Inherited family background

One's family background is a prominent virtue to possess for those aspiring to be hexagonal individuals. While previous generations greatly admired individuals who overcame challenging family environments and achieved success, today's generation admires those born with a gold spoon into affluent families from birth. The same applies to celebrity fandom. Older generations still passionately follow stories of individuals who endured hardships and finally achieved success through perseverance. For example, when a video of Lim Young-woong, who struggled with poverty, showed him winning a singing audition and presenting the trophy to his grandmother and mother, it quickly reached one million views. The tales of popular celebrities who have experienced poverty resonate with the middle-aged and older generations, who have also faced financial difficulties.

However, the younger generations have a different perspective. They praise idol members with phrases like, "so-and-so must have grown up in a good family; that's why their personality is so good." Do Woori, in her book *We Love Addiction*우리는 중독을 사랑해, notes that qualifiers such as "Gangnam-born," "received a good family upbringing," or "dad is a professor" have become commonplace descriptors for today's idols. Coming from a prosperous family background without any blemishes has become a selling point for them.

Influential figures that garner admiration have shifted from celebrities to individuals belonging to the third or fourth generation of chaebol families. For instance, Lee Joo-young, famously known as the "Daelim granddaughter," has gained popularity as a social media influencer with over 100,000 followers. She is the granddaughter of the honorary chairman of Daelim Group and currently attends a prestigious American university. Lee Joo-young is celebrated for showcasing her remarkable appearance, impeccable fashion sense, and active social engagements through her YouTube channel.

Another notable figure is Lee Won-ju, the daughter of Samsung Electronics executive chairman Lee Jae-yong. She frequently becomes the center of attention whenever she is in the media spotlight. For example, when she attends a fashion show alongside her mother, Lim Se-ryeong, who is the vice president of Daesang Group, the media is quick to capture images and report on their clothing brands, and their price tags. People intrigued by the daily lives of individuals from chaebol families eagerly follow their social media accounts to gain insights into their private lifestyles.

The current trend of "old money look" reflects people's admiration for their family's heritage and wealth. While the *nouveaux riches* often favor flashy, logo-heavy fashion to showcase their affluence, the traditionally affluent holders of old money prefer discreet logos and materials like cashmere, emanating an understated and refined style.

Many individuals appreciate this clean and sophisticated fashion style. For example, actress Gwyneth Paltrow gained significant attention in March 2023 for her timeless and refined old money look during a court appearance. The old money look is characterized by its reflection of a unique lifestyle, often incorporating elements from sports favored by the wealthy, such as horseback riding or yachting, as well as preppy styles inspired by uniforms from prestigious American private schools. This is why many members of Generation Z, aspiring to emulate an affluent appearance, are drawn to the old money look, regardless of their own wealth.

Natural appearance

The debate between a natural appearance and other factors like income or abilities has become more significant in recent times. For example, if we compare a man in the 80th percentile in terms of appearance with an annual salary of 60 million won against a man in the 20th percentile in looks but with an annual salary of 150 million won, who is more popular?

In February 2020, a survey asked this very question, pitting appearance and ability against one another. 52.1% of respondents chose "appearance." In the past, the belief that "for a man, appearance is temporary, while ability is permanent" was widely accepted. However, there is now a stronger tendency among people to think, "It's better to have outstanding looks than to excel in academics." It's important to note that appearance is largely a genetic attribute. While some individuals can enhance their appearance through plastic surgery or makeup, there are limitations to these efforts.

The inclination to prioritize appearance is not a new phenomenon; "lookism," which refers to an excessive preoccupation with one's appearance, has been around for some time. However, men's interest in their appearance has surged recently and is greater than ever before.

Men are increasingly becoming a significant presence in the fashion and beauty industries. According to an analysis by the market research service WiseApp·Retail·Goods, the number of male users on fashion apps like "Musinsa무신사" and "Kream크림" is steadily on the rise. Notably, the proportion of men in their twenties and their growth rate far surpass those of other age groups.

Furthermore, there is a growing male consumer base in the cosmetics market. Data released by CJ Olive Young in August 2023 reveals that the proportion of men among first-time customers has increased by 50% over the past three years. Men are diversifying their purchases in this market, moving beyond essential items like skincare and shaving products to include maintenance skincare products, tone-up sunscreen, colored lip balm, and hair treatments.

Among physical attributes, height is one that is particularly influenced by genetics. Surveys that equate the value of 1 cm in height to an annual salary in "millions of won" are frequently shared on online platforms. In a survey by online community Blind, 38% of respondents estimated the value of 1 cm in height to be 10 million won, 29% believed it to be between 10 to 50 million won, and surprisingly, 20% thought it was worth more than 100 million won. As more individuals consider height an important factor in the pursuit of a hexagonal image, an increasing number of people are taking measures to manage their height from a young age.

Data from the Health Insurance Assessment Service reveals that the number of children seeking medical attention due to concerns about short stature increased by approximately 50% in 2021 compared to 2016. This is a substantial growth rate, especially considering the declining birth rates each year. Many parents opt for costly treatments that are not covered by medical insurance. This decision is often driven by parental concerns about their children's height, even when there are no significant underlying health issues. They seek prescriptions for growth hormone injections before their children's growth plates close in hopes of increasing their height.

A naturally perfect character

Sometimes, innate attributes like "family origin" or "appearance" are pursued through a proxy. When it's challenging for an individual to become a hexagonal person themselves, they derive vicarious satisfaction by supporting celebrities or brands that embody these qualities. Analyzing social issue words related to the word "idol" from Conan Technology's social analysis, we observe a decrease in mentions of basic skills such as singing, acting, and dancing, which are traditionally expected from idols. In contrast, there is a gradual increase in mentions of appearance, personality, and family.

Being beloved by the public no longer hinges solely on an idol's exceptional abilities. Fans now hope that idols possess a well-rounded set of attributes. They expect idols to not only excel in their craft but also have good personalities, perform well academically, maintain a clean record regarding school violence, demonstrate proficiency in lyric-writing and composition, be multilingual, and come from a supportive family background. This multifaceted ideal is what fans commonly refer to as the "complete idol."

The desire for innate qualities is also evident in the content market. When we look at popular webtoons and comics from the past, many initially featured weak protagonists who underwent significant growth through their efforts. Whether it's Japanese manga like "Dragon Ball Z" and "One Piece," or Korean works like "Tower of God신의 탑" and "Noblesse노블

레스," these narratives typically revolved around a feeble hero becoming stronger and triumphing over formidable adversaries.

However, if we examine current webtoons like "I'm the only Max-Level Newbie나 혼자 만렙 뉴비," which currently ranks high in popularity on the Naver Webtoon platform, we see a different trend. These stories often skip or entirely eliminate the "suffering process." The main character's journey often begins with a dramatic twist, such as a car accident leading to reincarnation as a superpowered individual or a time jump to another era, resulting in a rebirth as a king. These stories present a fantastical life that unfolds with minimal effort. These immediately captivating narratives have garnered significant popularity. Even in the realm of content, there's a clear enthusiasm for protagonists who start with innate strength rather than relying on hard work and effort.

2. Quantification: Provide proof that you are a hexagonal individual

Dating reality shows like *Heart Signal*, *I'm SOLO*, *Exchange*, *Love Catcher*, *Single's Inferno*, *Change Days* have enjoyed popularity for several years, featuring everyday individuals showcasing their charms while searching for partners. What distinguishes these programs from the rest is the continuous evaluation of participants, not only by those appearing on the show but also by the viewers.

In the comments sections and related communities of these programs, viewers assign scores to various attributes, much like completing an evaluation table. Elements such as occupation, educational background, appearance, and personality are meticulously rated. To be acknowledged as hexagonal, people must convert these attributes into numerical values and provide supporting evidence.

Questions like these frequently appear on online community bulletin boards: "I am 35 years old, and my current assets amount to x million won, with a monthly salary of y million won. My house is rented, measuring z square meters, and I drive a XX brand car. What percentile do I belong to?" People seek recognition for their "well-being" by assessing their scores and social ranking within society based on these factors.

The emphasis on rankings and comparisons is pervasive among those aspiring to be hexagonal individuals. Instead of relying on subjective judgments like a neighborhood's atmosphere or the quality of public transportation, individuals might use tangible metrics like the price per square meter of a house to assess and compare their living situations. People often ask questions like, "My annual salary is only x won, can I buy a car at level z?" as a way to gauge their societal standing.

This desire to rank and compare is also projected onto one's favorite idols. In recent times, Korean idol group members have been fiercely competing to become brand ambassadors for luxury brands, leading to unexpected discussions about social class among fans. When an idol secures a coveted position as an ambassador for a prestigious luxury brand like Chanel or Louis Vuitton, it carries significant weight and importance. Fans often attach a sense of pride and achievement to their idol's ambassadorship, considering it not only a symbol of the idol's popularity but also an indicator of their status in the industry. However, the hierarchy doesn't stop there; within the brand, hierarchies are created based on factors like whether the idol is a global or domestic ambassador, what their role in cosmetics or fashion is, and whether they are invited to famous overseas fashion shows.

Converting values into money

In capitalist societies, money stands as the unequivocal cornerstone of value. Throughout human history, the importance of money has remained unwavering, yet in our present era, it serves as the ultimate metric for appraising all values. This transformation is particularly conspicuous in the realm of occupational preferences.

Traditionally, coveted occupations in Korean society included professions like doctor and lawyer, positions promising steadfast stability like teaching and civil service, and roles commanding influence in the market, such as executives in large corporations or CEOs of startups. In the past, it was commonplace for top-performing students on the nation's academic achievement tests^{학력고사} to pursue fields like electronic engineering or physics. However, contemporary trends have distilled this diversity down to one overarching pursuit: medical school.

Starting as early as elementary school, students enroll in specialized academies dedicated to securing admission to medical schools. Relentless competition ensues, as students with outstanding academic records vie for coveted positions within these institutions. Furthermore, there is a growing trend of individuals leaving their current professions to pursue careers in medicine, even to the extent of retaking the College Scholastic Ability Test (CSAT)^{대학수학능력시험}. This phenomenon can be attributed to a unique confluence of factors: a shrinking population, sluggish economic growth, and escalating uncertainty about the future. In this landscape, a doctor is esteemed as the epitome of stability and financial prosperity, making it an increasingly attractive choice.

The phenomenon of assessing individuals based on their wealth also manifests in the admiration of affluent lifestyles. Nowadays, the younger generations' fascination with wealthy individuals is more pronounced than ever. A case in point is Daniel Mac, a renowned American TikTok influencer, who has garnered approximately 14.3 million followers by creating videos where he encounters individuals driving supercars on the streets and inquires about their occupations.

The spectrum of occupations among supercar owners is notably diverse, spanning from CEOs of major corporations to actors and celebrities – even U.S. President Joe Biden – as well as lesser-known affluent individuals. In these videos, in addition to showcasing the extravagant prices of the supercars, Mac casually poses questions about the owners' professions, income, and advice for achieving success. This alone piques the curiosity and envy of viewers.

Entertainment programs offering viewers a vicarious glimpse into the extravagant lives of the wealthy have gained significant popularity. A prime example is a YouTube series that launched in June 2023 by ootb STUDIO, a multi-content production company, called "Sangpalja상팔자," meaning "good fortune" or "destined to be rich." In this show, a female comedian immerses herself directly in various VIP experiences typically reserved for the affluent. She crashes exclusive lounges frequented by department store VIP customers and indulges in hotel suites at nearly 20 million won per night.

Viewers have responded enthusiastically, appreciating the relatability of an ordinary person experiencing these luxurious amenities. They've noted, "It's even more enjoyable because you're someone who wouldn't normally have access to such experiences." Each episode consistently amasses well over a million views. "Sangpalja" delivers a unique form of vicarious satisfaction, democratizing access to services that were previously the exclusive privilege of the wealthy. It allows the public to partake in the luxuries of a hexagonal life that were once beyond their reach.

3. Hexagonal play: Making fun of desire through play

There is a way to take selfies that is popular among "nuclear insiders핵인싸" (people who are extremely trendy and get along well with others in a group) these days. When the main character poses and people around them take out their smartphones and pretend to film the main character, the entire scene is captured in one cut. It creates an appearance similar to being bombarded with camera flashes by the paparazzi on the red carpet. Even if you are an ordinary person who has never stood on a red carpet in your life, you may sometimes dream of becoming the main character in a movie. To borrow an expression from people in their 20s these days, who attach "material재질" to specific situations and characters, such as "princess material," "romance comic material," or "first love material," we could call nuclear insiders "main character material." However, just as there is only one main character in a novel, not all members of society can be the main character at every moment. Likewise, everyone dreams of becoming a hexagon individual, but not many people can actually achieve it. Is there anyone in the world who is so perfect? However, you cannot just give up entirely. So, how should we solve this dilemma? One way might be: "If you can't avoid it, enjoy it." The reality of hexagonalism's unobtainability is caricaturized and laughed off, like a game.

It is also popular to exaggerate ordinary reality and act as if you are a great person. Recently, taking graduation photos wearing a princess dress has become popular among middle and high school female students. As web novels and webtoons in the romance fantasy genre become popular, people imitate the main characters in the content. As of August 2023, 6 out of the top 15 works in Naver Web Novel's integrated rankings and 4 works in the top 10 popular rankings in Kakao Webtoon fall into the romance fantasy genre. Romance fantasy works are often set in the Middle Ages, and the main characters are generally nobles or royals. Because servants usually refer to high-status female protagonists as "young-ae영애" – esteemed daughter – the costumes worn by female protagonists are often called "young-ae concept dresses." Wearing a princess dress will not actually make you a princess, but students enjoy feeling like princesses, even if only for a moment.

Sometimes, exaggerating and pretending to be a hexagonal person can lead to unexpected results. "Girl Girl Oranceee걸걸오랜씨," a girl group of ordinary elementary school students who pretend to be idols and eventually become real idols, is such a case. The name of the three-member girl group, which debuted in July 2023, does not even appear when searched for on internet news. Neither does their music pop up when searching with a sound clip on music sites such as Melon멜론. So, can we even call them "idols"? In fact, these are not idols who officially debuted through a production company. Their debut was a video posted on Instagram, no different from other ordinary elementary school students uploading videos and calling themselves "idols." But rather than becoming a silly meme, they consistently uploaded photos and Reels to Instagram, imitating idols quite well and going viral in the process. As of September 2023, their Instagram following is close to 19,000, and a fandom named "OA오아" was recently created. Even another group of ordinary people, "Girl Girl Uncle걸걸아저씨", which parodied them, popped up. The desire to become a hexagonal human appears everywhere in society, regardless of gender or age.

The infinitely positive attitude of shouting, "I will always be successful!" is also a way to overcome the pressure of becoming a hexagonal person. In the first half of 2023, videos containing the hashtag #luckygirlsyndrome recorded over 100 million views on TikTok. The lucky girl syndrome is a type of optimistic "self-persuasion" craze in which people believe that good things will happen if you repeatedly shout out how lucky you are, even if evidence is lacking.

Background: The Rise of Social Perfectionism Among Younger Generations

A study conducted by psychologist Dr. Thomas Curran and his research team, involving more than 40,000 students across the United States, United Kingdom, and Canada, has shed light on a growing trend, particularly among the younger generations. This trend is the belief that one must present an image of perfection to gain recognition, a phenomenon referred to as "social perfectionism."

According to the research findings, young people today increasingly feel the pressure to excel in social situations. They believe that they must project an image of flawless achievement because they perceive that others are evaluating them more critically. The researchers provide insight into this shift, stating that young individuals are becoming more acutely aware of the social dynamics at play around them. In response to heightened scrutiny, these individuals feel compelled to project an image of greater perfection to garner acceptance.

Unlike previous generations, today's youth have grown up in an era marked by significantly higher economic standards. They have also received extensive self-esteem training, emphasizing the importance of self-worth. However, despite these advantages, the expectation of perfection persists. Why is this the case?

First, erecting walls of stringent, unobtainable standards that define hexagonal individuals is closely intertwined with the erosion of the "social ladder." This phenomenon has become increasingly pronounced amid heightened wealth polarization, catalyzed by events like the global financial crisis of 2008 and the coronavirus pandemic in 2020. During these crises, the conventional belief in the "myth of hard work노력신화" – the notion that individual exertion alone dictates success – has started to crumble.

Korean society, rooted in principles of individualism and meritocracy, has long espoused the idea that one's destiny hinges entirely on individual effort. Nevertheless, in contemporary times, this faith in the attainability of success through sheer personal toil is waning. According to a social analysis by Konan Technology, twenty and thirty-somethings in Korea exhibit a pronounced inclination toward viewing success as a product of inherent assets such as intelligence, education, and talent. As the path of upward mobility becomes increasingly arduous, the value of effort itself is undergoing a profound reassessment. In the void left by the fading myth of hard work, attributes that are intrinsic, including family background, physical appearance, and natural talent – qualities not easily acquired by everyone – are beginning to take precedence.

The waning influence of the myth of hard work in modern society is closely tied to the growing number of wealthy individuals who have amassed riches beyond what is commonly perceived as an "insurmountable wall." This wall represents a level of affluence that goes far beyond what can be achieved through diligent effort alone; it stands as an unattainable pinnacle. In an era where a single technology or platform can dominate the global market, the pace at which tech tycoons amass fortunes and the sheer magnitude of their wealth have reached astronomical proportions, rendering their accomplishments virtually unimaginable and unattainable for ordinary individuals. This goes beyond mere comparison; it becomes increasingly challenging to even harbor envy. In such a landscape, personal efforts may indeed begin to feel overwhelmingly insignificant.

Secondly, the phenomenon of assigning grades to others through comparison and establishing one's worth in quantifiable terms is intimately intertwined with the rise of social media. The advent of social media has not only facilitated the process of comparing ourselves with others but has also normalized these comparisons.

We're constantly comparing ourselves to others, checking our social media feeds every minute and second for bright, pretty, and over-the-top images. The circle of comparison has expanded. Comparisons that used to be between friends and neighbors now extend to celebrity influencers who have nothing to do with us. As we peek into other people's lives, the size of our desires grows larger and larger. With more criteria and more people to compare ourselves to, we naturally start to score and grade each other.

"The graduate school I was accepted to was ranked #1 in the world in my major, so of course I decided to go there. However, since that university is somewhat unfamiliar in Korea...... In addition, I simultaneously applied to other graduate schools that are widely known to Koreans and received several acceptance letters. I wanted my abilities to be recognized by people who didn't know much about the graduate school I was going to. Also, people may say that I was lucky if I only got accepted to one school, but I think being accepted to multiple graduate schools proves that my skills are real. In particular, people in my field communicate through LinkedIn or Instagram, so it was important to post various graduate school acceptance certificates on social media."

- Consumer Trend Insight team's own interview

For individuals striving to attain the status of a hexagonal individual, the presentation of their scores and rankings on social media platforms holds significance. In the interview mentioned earlier, a male student in his twenties, preparing to study abroad, submitted an admission application to another graduate school where he had no intention of enrolling, even incurring additional fees. His sole purpose was to obtain an acceptance certificate, which he promptly shared on social media. The driving force behind this decision was a desire for proper recognition and evaluation by his peers and the wider online community.

In the world of these individuals, daily social media posts serve as a type of personal portfolio. These posts not only share their accomplishments but also invite scrutiny and appraisal from their social circles. This continuous exhibition of achievements becomes a means of establishing credibility, fostering a reputation, and garnering recognition from others, further fueling their pursuit of excellence and hexagonal status.

Outlook and Implications

The hexagonal human has become a coveted ideal among today's youth, representing a desire for success and recognition. However, it's worth considering that this hexagon may be more of a societal construct than a personal dream.

When one ponders where the epitome of hexagonal individuals resides in Korea, Gangnam in Seoul naturally comes to mind. However, the perspective of a psychiatrist who has closely observed Gangnam differs from this common perception. Dr. Kim Jong-il김정일, who has operated a psychiatric clinic in Gangnam for 28 years, recently authored a book titled *Gangnam is a Huge Psychiatric Ward*강남은 거대한 정신

병동이다. He chose this title because he believes Gangnam is a place where many of the underlying issues plaguing Korean society are most prominently exposed. These issues include the pervasive sense of inferiority stemming from intense competition, materialism, class consciousness, and an excessive emphasis on education. It's crucial to recognize that labeling Gangnam as "problematic" is not the point. Dr. Kim's viewpoint serves as a reminder that even in places celebrated as models of success and "hexagonality," individuals still grapple with the societal pressures and challenges that afflict our broader society. This underscores that the pursuit of the hexagonal ideal, while attractive, does not shield individuals from the inherent difficulties and complexities of contemporary life.

Amidst the prevalent culture of excessive comparison and the pressures of conforming to societal ideals, a countermovement has emerged: a quest to discover one's true self and liberate oneself from the scrutinizing gaze and desires of others. This movement seeks to redefine the role of social media, shifting it from a source of self-destruction and distortion through ceaseless comparison into a constructive tool for authentic self-expression.

In response to the invisible tyranny often propagated by social media, particularly among Generation Z, there is a growing trend of people sharing their daily lives with a more limited audience. Many are opting to make their posts private, restricting access to only close friends and connections, and directing their interactions primarily through direct messages (DMs) rather than posting publicly.

Moreover, the approach to sharing photos on social media is evolving. There's a rising trend where it's considered trendy to post a collection of photos depicting daily life, rather than a meticulously crafted single "life shot." This practice is commonly referred to as a "photo dump." As of September 2023, there have been over 3.5 million posts on Instagram featuring the hashtag #photodump, while TikTok videos with the same hashtag have collectively garnered over 3 billion views.

The rise of private social media platforms and the popularity of photo dumps could be indicative of social media fatigue. In recent times, there has been a gradual decline in the user base of platforms like Facebook and X (formerly Twitter). Whereas annual user increases once reached as high as 400 to 500 million in the late 2010s, projections now suggest a decrease to 200 million starting from 2024. This shift underscores a potential shift in user preferences and a growing weariness with conventional social media platforms.

The phenomenon of hexagonal humans, where comparison, the pursuit of perfection, and even playful competition take center stage, can indeed be entertaining. However, it's crucial to acknowledge the heavy burden that comes with striving to conform to society's expectations of a hexagonal person.

Previous generations, who weathered challenging times, often ask young people questions like, "What are you lacking?" These inquiries reflect a desire to understand the younger generations' experiences. However, it's equally important to recognize that within their own generation, there exists the stress of fierce competition and the pressure of self-censorship, ultimately leading to the pursuit of an ideal figure akin to the hexagonal human.

The core reason people envy hexagonal individuals is the belief that becoming one would lead to happiness. When are we at our happiest? It might sound cliché, but isn't it when we are at our personal best, even if it's not a perfect hexagon? True happiness often emerges when we are true to ourselves and thriving in our own unique ways, rather than chasing an idealized image of perfection.

Getting the Price Right:
Variable Pricing

There is no such thing as a single price. The 19th-century British economist William Stanley Jevons argued for the "Law of Indifference," which states that there can be only one price for the same commodity and no price discrimination. For a long time, we have been producing, selling, and buying on the premise that "one thing has a fixed price." The concepts of "list price" and "recommended retail price" are examples of this. Today, this premise is breaking down. As pricing policies in the market become more complex, they are becoming a new tool for demand promotion and marketing. *Consumer Trend Insights 2024* proposes the keyword "variable pricing strategy" with the idea that the same product can be priced differently depending on when, where, who, and how it is bought, and that suppliers and distributors can consider pricing a strategy.

"Price," in a nutshell, is "value perceived by the customer." The same product is valued differently to different people in different situations. So, when do consumers perceive the value of the same product differently? In this chapter, we will examine the following factors: (1) time of purchase; (2) channel of purchase; (3) consumer characteristics; (4) options, which are ways to sell products; and (5) a broader variable pricing strategy that comprehensively considers all of these factors, known as "dynamic pricing."

In order to implement a successful variable pricing strategy, it is necessary to build a price control tower that can respond agilely to various market changes. Furthermore, it is important to recognize both the power and limitations of the pricing strategy and to present price differentiation that is acceptable to consumers. It is hoped that various price differentiations will not only maximize the profits of producers and distributors, but also enhance the purchase value for consumers, thereby reconciling corporate growth and consumer welfare.

In 1999, Coca-Cola installed temperature sensors in their vending machines and introduced a pricing strategy that raised prices on hot days and lowered them on cold days. This ambitious vending machine project, initially expecting a sales increase of over 20%, ultimately failed due to strong consumer opposition. However, this episode prompts contemplation. It challenges the conventional notion that a can of soda should always cost the same, regardless of when or where it's purchased, suggesting that even within the same vending machine, prices can vary.

The "Law of Indifference" put forth by 19th-century British economist William Stanley Jevons asserted that identical products should share a uniform price, precluding any form of price discrimination. We have long operated on the assumption (though not strictly observed), that "one product has one fixed price." This concept has given rise to notions like "list price" or "recommended retail price." However, this foundational premise is beginning to erode. In the aviation market, there's the principle: "Even on the same plane, the price of each seat differs." Depending on the time and route chosen by consumers, the prospect of paying different prices for identical products and services has become more prevalent.

The price of the same product can vary significantly depending on when, where, how, and by whom it's purchased, and suppliers and distributors can strategically set these prices. We refer to this approach as a "variable pricing strategy." This strategy involves a methodology that can generate demand that previously may not have existed by presenting a multitude of various prices rather than a single fixed price. Thanks to the variable pricing strategy, the market paradigm is shifting from the traditional "one price for one product" model to "numerous prices for one product."

Pricing differentiation policies, such as early morning discounts or student discounts that we are accustomed to, are not a recent phenomenon. However, in recent years, the emergence of innovative pricing strategies rooted in behavioral economics and the utilization of big data have ushered in an entirely new era for pricing policies. In their book *Marketing 4.0*, marketing experts Philip Kotler, Hermawan Kartajaya, and Iwan Setiawan astutely observed the highly adaptable nature of pricing in the digital age. As traditional, standardized, and fixed pricing gradually gives way to dynamic approaches, it has evolved into an outstanding marketing tool.

Consequently, pricing is emerging as a pivotal subject.

With costs escalating and profit margins dwindling amid record inflation, producers and distributors find themselves in need of innovative solutions. Simultaneously, consumers must devise strategies to efficiently allocate their limited resources. In this evolving landscape, a range of pricing strategies is emerging as appealing options for both businesses and consumers. Let's explore various instances of wise pricing strategies that can fulfill the needs of both consumers and companies.

Transitioning from a Single Price to a Variety of Prices

Adam Smith likened the setting of prices to an "invisible hand" that guides the market economy. When this invisible hand operates, prices naturally settle at the point where supply and demand converge, making it a commonplace phenomenon for a single product to have a uniform price. Producers and sellers took this singular price as a given and focused on methods to maximize their profits. It's possible that this is why, among the 4P strategies encompassing Product, Price, Promotion, and Place, pricing strategy historically received relatively less attention from marketers.

However, with the advancement of information technologies like big data and artificial intelligence, there is now a technical possibility to measure an individual's "willingness to pay" (WTP, the highest amount that a consumer is willing to spend to acquire a particular product or service) – a concept previously regarded as a black box. This shift marks a significant departure from the traditional approach of having one fixed price for a product.

Pricing has evolved into a potent marketing tool and a significant source of profit generation. Consequently, a single product can now have a multitude of n different prices.

Traditional pricing approaches have typically been supplier-centric, but variable pricing takes a different approach by prioritizing the consumer's perspective over the supplier's. To accommodate the varying levels of willingness of individual consumers to pay, diverse price points are established based on the perceived value from the consumer's standpoint. Predictive models consider an array of variables including the timing of the purchase, the location, and the buyer's unique characteristics, allowing for prices to be determined at each interaction point accordingly.

Variable Pricing Strategy: Exploring Different Dimensions

In his book *Confessions of the Pricing Man: How Price Affects Everything*, renowned pricing expert Hermann Simon succinctly defines "price" as "the value felt by the customer." The perceived value of the same product can vary significantly depending on the circumstances and the individual. For instance, a consumer's perception of the value of an amusement park ticket on a sunny day might differ from that on a cloudy day. When consumers attribute higher value to a product, demand tends to rise, which can lead to price increases. Ultimately, the key to diversifying prices hinges on understanding the value perceived by consumers.

We will delve into five criteria that influence how consumers perceive the value of the same item differently:

1. Time: The timing of the product purchase.
2. Channel: The channel or platform through which the product is purchased.
3. Consumer Characteristics: The unique characteristics and preferences of the buyer.
4. Options: The various methods used to sell a product.
5. Dynamic Pricing: A comprehensive strategy that considers the above factors and encompasses a broad range of pricing approaches.

1.Time: Adjusting prices over time

The element of time is a critical variable that influences a product's perceived value among consumers. When contemplating price diversification strategies, time is typically the first variable that comes to mind.

Firstly, during periods of reduced demand, often referred to as the "off-season," prices can be lowered to stimulate demand. This approach is especially effective in brick-and-mortar stores with limited capacity, where setting different prices based on time and the season is a common practice to enhance operational efficiency. An illustrative example is the concept of "happy hour" in restaurants. A notable success story is the British luxury restaurant Bob Bob Ricard, which has adopted a unique flexible pricing model. This establishment offers the same menu items at a 25% discount on off-peak Mondays, a 15% discount on "mid-peak" Tuesdays and Sundays, and at regular prices on other days of the week. What distinguishes this strategy from others is the discreet nature of these varying prices. High-end restaurants, mindful of their clientele and special occasions, refrain from displaying discounted prices on their menus to uphold the dignity of their patrons. Instead, patrons appreciate the delightful surprise of dining at a lower cost during unadvertised discount periods.

In certain instances, prices follow a downward trajectory over time. This method involves launching a new product with a high list price to capture the initial wave of eager consumers, followed by gradual reductions to attract subsequent customer segments. It is predominantly employed in markets characterized by exceptional technological advancements or product differentiations. At first glance, this approach may resemble depreciation, but it closely aligns with tracking the demand curve, which represents varying levels of willingness to pay among individual consumers over an extended period. This is commonly known as a "skimming strategy."

A notable example is Apple's approach with their iPhone product line. Apple typically sets a high initial launch price for iPhones to signal innovation and attract early adopters and loyal customers. After several months, they systematically reduce the price to stimulate broader demand. For instance, the iPhone 13 Mini, initially released at 946,000 won in October 2021, was subsequently discounted to approximately 230,000 won, equivalent to a 75% discount off the initial price, in August 2023. This strategy effectively captures the remaining demand for existing smartphones before the introduction of the next new iPhone series.

In the digital media field, a "pay or wait기다리면 무료" strategy is being used, in which content is provided for free over time. For example, in a mobile game, you can play the game for free if you wait a certain amount of time, but if you want to play the game right away without waiting, you have to pay a price. This strategy is also actively used in webtoons and web novels. Naver Webtoon uploads one webtoon every week, and you can view it for free if you wait 24 hours. However, if you want to preview the work that will be uploaded next week, you must pay a fee called a "cookie."

Real-time pricing fluctuations are becoming increasingly prevalent, extending beyond the airline and lodging industries. In sectors like these, prices typically rise as the date of use approaches; but a day before, they often undergo substantial drops, resulting in significant price volatility. This phenomenon is now expanding to encompass other industries as well.

From a company's perspective, the ability to adjust prices in real time poses a unique challenge. While it can potentially boost profits, missteps in this area can undermine price stability and attract criticism from the public. For instance, Tesla has gained notoriety for its frequent price adjustments. In 2022, prices soared to unprecedented levels, leading to the adage, "Buying today is the cheapest." However, in 2023, the company shifted its strategy to continuously lower prices due to a decline in market demand. This approach resulted in instances where customers in China, having already signed contracts, protested at Tesla stores demanding refunds after prices were reduced by 10 million won, even before they received their vehicles.

2. Channel: Where did you buy that?

Prices also vary depending on the distribution channel of the product. For instance, a Coke can cost 1,700 won at a convenience store but balloons to 5,000 won at a hotel minibar. Likewise, the price of ice cream varies based on the point of sale. Take 'Melona메로나' ice cream, for example; it is available for 1,500 won at convenience stores, 1,200 won at large supermarkets, 600 won at unmanned stores, and 1,000 won at Daiso다이소.

Lately, in online communities frequented by newlyweds, one can come across individuals exclaiming, "I've finally graduated from home appliances!" When you manage to acquire a desired home appliance at a favorable price, it brings about a sense of achievement, pride, and relief, akin to graduating. Couples preparing for marriage must acquire an assortment of home appliances all at once, but the prices can fluctuate significantly depending on whether they are shopping at a department store, supermarket, or flagship store. That's why online forums sometimes share price information about a "sanctuary성지," saying that the place sells something at the cheapest price they've seen today. And it's not just for home appliances: when traveling abroad, people are busy searching for the platform that offers the cheapest accommodations for booking, and sharing methods to snag bookings at the lowest price. For example, it is cheaper to pay through Google Maps rather than directly through online travel agency Agoda.

Following this, price comparison services, which traditionally focused on identifying the lowest-priced sellers on e-commerce platforms, have recently expanded their scope to encompass all aspects of daily life. One such example is the mobile app "Oil Now오일나우," which, in collaboration with the Korea National Oil Corporation, collects real-time information on gas stations nationwide and recommends the cheapest gas station based on the driver's current location. Additionally, there are apps that compare prices for personal training sessions at nearby gyms and the fees for driving lessons, which are widely popular.

A recent development in the realm of pricing strategies, driven by channel diversity, is the practice of manufacturers selling directly to consumers through their own websites, known as "D2C" (Direct to Consumer). D2C channels offer several advantages, including cost reduction and increased direct interactions with consumers. Consequently, many manufacturers are investing in establishing their own direct sales channels, even at the expense of initial setup costs. While companies with intricate distribution networks may encounter resistance from existing distribution partners when implementing D2C policies, this approach remains an appealing pricing strategy for brand manufacturers. Consumers are also drawn to D2C as it allows them to access the same products at more affordable prices.

An example of rapid growth through a D2C channel is Lululemon, a globally recognized sportswear brand. Historically, many sportswear companies primarily relied on supplying large retailers to drive sales. However, Lululemon has strategically expanded its sales by bolstering its online channels. Consequently, the company's direct sales, encompassing both online and offline avenues, now exceed 90%, with over 40% of total sales originating from its online store.

One notable advantage of activating D2C channels is the ability to gather detailed data on customers' buying patterns and preferences. This invaluable information enables companies to offer tailored products and services to their customers. Moreover, consistent personalized communication with customers each time they visit an online store helps foster a strong brand-customer relationship.

In the manufacturing sector, Samsung Electronics has recently demonstrated a proactive pursuit of a D2C strategy. In December 2022, Samsung Electronics established a D2C center within its Global Marketing Office to enhance sales through its online store. It has also shown flexibility by adjusting prices in response to price fluctuations among competing retailers through their own website, which operates in multiple countries. Consequently, online sales of Samsung Electronics' home appliance division have steadily risen since surpassing 22% of total sales for the first time in 2020. Furthermore, Samsung expanded its dedicated e-store for business-to-business (B2B) customers to 30 countries worldwide, achieving nearly double the sales compared to the same period in the previous year.

3. Consumer characteristics: Prices just for you

Observing consumer characteristics is a strategy that leverages various data, including customer demographics and purchasing behaviors. New customers are one of the most crucial customer segments for a company. Attracting new customers is challenging, but there's a significant potential for them to become loyal customers in the future. This is especially true in the "subscription business" model, where continuous purchases are made after signing up. Offering an unprecedented price to entice new customers becomes paramount. A notable example of this approach can be seen in the domestic music platform Melon, which generated buzz by providing new customers with a two-month unlimited listening pass for just 100 won. This strategy aimed to secure more monthly users in a highly competitive music market. Similar practices occur offline as well, with local beauty salons and nail shops frequently offering discounted services to first-time customers. Some even refer to this phenomenon as "beauty shop drifting," where individuals seek discounts solely on their initial visit.

In the e-commerce industry, where customer purchase data accumulates as significant big data, the spotlight is on personalized pricing strategies tailored to individual customers. Online retailer, Kurly컬리, is distributing "secret coupons" accompanied by personalized messages like "Coupons exclusively for you!" This approach is considered effective in re-engaging customers who haven't visited recently. Furthermore, target customer segments can be defined with, say, beef discount coupons going to customers with a history of purchasing beef, or electronic product-related discounts offered to those with a history of buying electronic goods. Kurly is dedicated to reducing customer churn rates and boosting conversion rates through hyper-personalized, customized marketing efforts.

In this manner, strategies aimed at existing customers make active use of customer behavior data available within the company's platform. Data generated from the company's online store, including customer visit records, shopping cart details, and payment histories, are commonly referred to as "first-party cookies." Pricing strategies employing these data sets have gained prominence in recent times. This shift is primarily attributed to the increasing limitations on third-party cookies, which can track user behavior across different websites, owing to data privacy regulations. Notably, global internet browser giants such as Apple's Safari and Google's Chrome have initiated restrictions on third-party cookies, with a comprehensive phase-out of these cookies anticipated for 2024. Consequently, Customer Relationship Management (CRM) marketing, which facilitates intricate and comprehensive customer management grounded in first-party cookies, is once again garnering significant attention.

Individual prices can vary significantly through partnerships with other companies. Typically, financial institutions leverage data from "T-Map Mobility" to offer unique benefits to their customers. Among these partnerships, one of the most noteworthy is the collaboration with insurance companies that provide auto insurance.

When a consumer utilizes T-Map's navigation function and drives a certain distance, T-Map analyzes their driving habits and calculates a safe driving score. Insurance companies offer reduced insurance premiums to consumers who achieve a score exceeding a specified threshold, indicating responsible driving habits. These discounts can go as high as 13%. Several insurance providers, including Samsung Fire & Marine Insurance삼성화재, KB InsuranceKB손해보험, and Hyundai Marine & Fire Insurance현대해상, have embraced this approach, expanding their specialized offerings for targeted customer segments. Looking ahead, it's anticipated that driver data will play a role in credit evaluation when individuals apply for new loans.

We are currently entering an era characterized by hyper-personalized pricing, where every consumer is presented with unique price offers. Correspondingly, services related to this trend are gaining prominence. G Market, for instance, has recently introduced a "hyper-personalized price comparison service" that tailors its recommendations based on individual consumer profiles when searching for products. Even customers exhibiting similar purchasing behavior can receive significantly varied price offers, depending on the discount coupons they possess and whether they have a membership.

This innovative service takes into account all available coupons that customers can apply and strategically showcases products with the "genuine lowest price" by placing them at the top of the recommendations. Following the introduction of this service, click efficiency has improved by 20% compared to the previous system, contributing to heightened product visibility and increased sales.

4. Options: Only pay for what you spend

Luna-X루나엑스, situated in Gyeongju, stands out as a golf course with a unique twist. Offering four distinct 6-hole courses, players can choose to engage in rounds of 6, 12, 18, or 24 holes, with the added convenience of locker rooms and shower facilities based on their preferences. The absence of reception counters and sheltered areas, along with the use of automated carts instead of caddies, translates to significantly reduced prices. According to the Korea Leisure Industry Research Institute, Luna-X ranks as the third most affordable golf course for weekend rounds in the country. Remarkably, despite the cost savings, the course layout promises an enjoyable experience, and the fairways and greens remain in impeccable condition thanks to drone-based management. As in the case of Luna-X, a method in which individual consumers can select what they want and pay only the corresponding costs is called "unbundled pricing." "Bundled pricing," on the other hand, is selling the basic product and optional features at a combined price, like at existing golf courses.

The pricing strategy based on options is a non-combined pricing policy that tailors prices based on a range of available features or usage levels. While originally prevalent in the software market, this strategy has now extended its reach into various industries. Particularly during economic downturns, there is a growing consumer preference for purchasing precisely what one needs. By offering a diverse array of options, businesses can not only attract new customers but also satisfy the desire for price competitiveness among consumers.

With the proliferation of low-cost airlines entering the market, options pricing strategies have become increasingly prevalent within the airline industry. Rather than reducing the base ticket price, airlines are now applying additional charges for services such as checked baggage, early boarding, and in-flight meals. Even within the same economy class, ticket prices are segmented into different tiers with varying fees. For instance, Asiana Airlines offers "Economy Smartium" seats, which boast an extra 4 inches of width between the seats in the same economy class. They also provide legroom seats that offer approximately 16 centimeters of extra legroom. These Smartium seats are available for long-distance routes, such as those to the Americas or Europe, but come with an additional fee of around 200,000 won per one-way ticket.

Other examples include Jeju Air, which provides a priority baggage service for a supplementary fee of 3,000 to 5,000 won, ensuring faster baggage delivery. And Turkish Airlines offers a "No Kids Zone," where children are not allowed to sit, for an additional fee of 45 euros when reserving a seat.

These practices exemplify the growing adoption of options pricing strategies in the airline industry, allowing passengers to customize their travel experiences according to their preferences and budgets.

Option-specific pricing strategies aren't limited to large corporations. A restaurant in Seoul once garnered attention for including charges for replacing spoons (1,000 won), chopsticks (200 won), and small plates (1,000 won) on its menu. Additionally, they had specified costs for glass breakage and for any incidents resulting in contamination within the establishment, including vomit. Consumer reactions to these pricing details, however, were mixed.

Initially, most consumers found the pricing structure to be absurd. However, opinions shifted when the restaurant's menu revealed that beer and soju were priced ridiculously low at around 2,000 won. This disclosure prompted some to defend the restaurant's approach, with arguments such as, "Considering the low food prices, it's reasonable," and "Customers who frequently drop their spoons should be responsible for the replacement costs."

This is the core of the options pricing strategy. To quell customer complaints asking, "Do you charge extra for that?", the basic price must be low while maintaining core capabilities of the product or service.

5. Price as the ultimate factor: The variable pricing strategy

Up until now, we've delved into elements like time, distribution channels, customer characteristics, and options as fundamental factors influencing pricing strategies. However, for the sake of clarity, let's provide a more comprehensive explanation.

In today's real-world market, a multitude of factors come into play when setting prices. These include factors such as demand, production costs, profit margins, competitor pricing trends, and even external variables like weather conditions, events, and emerging trends. Theoretically, prices that dynamically adjust in response to these multifaceted influences are termed "dynamic pricing" or "dynamic pricing strategies." In a broader sense, this approach can be encompassed under the umbrella of a "variable pricing strategy."

The variable pricing strategy has become a global trend, with Amazon serving as a prime example. Since 2012, Amazon has implemented a policy of continuously adjusting prices in real-time, keeping a watchful eye on customer demand, product costs, and competitor pricing. Remarkably, it's reported that Amazon changes its product prices a staggering 2.5 million times per day.

Amazon's strategy is multi-faceted. For products with lower price sensitivity, the company raises prices slightly to secure higher margins. Conversely, for items with higher price sensitivity, Amazon aggressively reduces prices, aiming to create the perception among consumers that Amazon offers cost-effective options.

Many Korean companies are increasingly embracing the variable pricing strategy, especially within the competitive landscape of the e-commerce market, where price wars are a daily occurrence. Real-time price adjustments have become a prevalent practice.

For instance, Coupang has taken cues from Amazon's approach and actively employs dynamic pricing. When other platforms lower their prices, Coupang swiftly follows suit with price reductions. In response to this pricing strategy, consumers have turned to apps that notify them of price fluctuations. "Fallcent," a notification app that alerts users to price drops on Coupang Rocket Delivery products, offers daily price updates based on factors such as membership status and the type of payment card used. Users can also set alerts for their desired price points.

Furthermore, SSG.com recently introduced in 2023 a price optimization AI service. Instead of sellers manually adjusting prices individually, this AI service automates the process, taking into account product attributes, order data, and external pricing data to create an optimized price that changes daily.

The ticket pricing for the NC Dinos, a professional baseball team, has recently become a widely discussed topic due to its AI-driven system developed by parent company NCSoft's "NLP Center." As of 2022, the baseball stadium offered six ticket types, with prices varying by weekday/ weekend, or child/adult. However, since the introduction of AI, the number of ticket categories has expanded significantly, reaching as many as 85 variations. For instance, even the cheapest ticket in outfield block number 133 is priced at 1,800 won. This is quite remarkable, especially when considering that the most affordable children's ticket on a weekday at Jamsil Baseball Stadium in Seoul starts at 3,000 won.

Dynamic pricing has recently found its way into brick-and-mortar stores, thanks to the advent of electronic shelf labels (ESL). These labels enable businesses to adjust prices to their desired rates effortlessly, eliminating the need for frequent paper price tag replacements. ESL is an automated system that employs a wireless network to update and display real-time product information, including shelf prices and barcodes, within the store.

Thanks to thriving market growth, "SoluM솔루엠," a domestic ESL sales company, achieved its best-ever performance in the second quarter of 2023. Operating profit surged by an impressive 111% compared to the same period in the previous year, surpassing market expectations and doubling the anticipated results.

Background: Emergence of the Variable Pricing Strategy

The adoption of the variable pricing strategy is primarily attributed to the evolving market dynamics. In essence, with the advancement of IT technology, consumers' access to pricing information has increased, while the influence of value-driven consumption has grown significantly. This has underscored the importance of AI-powered pricing functions, capable of real-time calculations involving numerous variables.

A survey conducted by the consulting firm BCG, encompassing 1,400 global price decision makers, revealed that 70% of respondents anticipate ongoing uncertainties in the medium term, including factors like inflation, economic recessions, and market volatility. Additionally, 63% expressed concerns about potential declines in both profits and sales volumes. In response to the heightened need for flexible pricing strategies in light of persisting market uncertainties, companies are expediting their transition toward predictive pricing models that proactively respond to shifts in demand, rather than merely reacting through price hikes.

Of particular note is the recent surge in inflation rates, which has led to rapid cost escalation across various sectors. However, indiscriminate price increases can impose a substantial burden on companies. Such increases typically lead to reduced consumer spending, triggering backlash from consumers, and often prompting government interventions aimed at stabilizing prices. In this challenging context, if price adjustments are inevitable, a win-win pricing policy that identifies a mutually acceptable pricing equilibrium with consumers becomes imperative.

One crucial aspect contributing to the adoption of variable pricing strategies is the emergence of groundbreaking products. Historically, companies often adjusted their pricing strategies by benchmarking against average market prices and comparing their prices with those of competitors. However, in a market where products and services are continually evolving towards unprecedented innovations, more and more companies are faced with the challenge of pricing these unique offerings. In such situations, there are no reference points from competitors' prices, and determining prices solely based on production costs becomes an intricate task. Consumers, too, find it difficult to assess whether a service or product they are encountering for the first time represents good value or is expensive. In these scenarios, adopting a variable pricing approach that fluctuates over time proves to be more advantageous than a fixed pricing model focused solely on profit maximization.

Notably, many of the examples of variable pricing strategies mentioned earlier have become feasible due to the rise of the platform economy. The effective implementation of a well-structured variable pricing strategy demands a wealth of detailed information, particularly a comprehensive understanding of consumers' willingness to pay. With the advent of the platform economy, companies have gained the ability to quantify and record various consumer purchasing behaviors. Furthermore, advancements in AI technology have ushered in the era of "hyper-personalization of prices," enabling the provision of dozens of personalized price points for a single product. This trend is rapidly gaining momentum in today's marketplace.

Outlook and Implications

Establishing a price control tower

Hermann Simon's book, *Confessions of the Pricing Man*, underscores the profound impact that pricing strategies have on profits and highlights the need for top corporate executives to prioritize pricing matters. However, it is concerning that a significant majority of companies do not seem to share this perspective. According to the Professional Pricing Society (PPS), a mere 5% of Fortune 500 companies have a dedicated department responsible for pricing decisions. These findings reveal that, despite the clear correlation between pricing and a company's sales, many businesses continue to approach pricing from a subjective standpoint.

Companies that excel in pricing strategies invariably have CEOs who place a high value on this critical aspect of their business. Specifically, to implement an outstanding variable pricing strategy, it is imperative to continually monitor and promptly respond to a myriad of variables, including market fluctuations, consumer feedback, competitive actions, and inventory levels. To effectively navigate this dynamic environment, establishing the company's own "price control tower" becomes vital. McKinsey advises that during times of escalating prices, the pace of decision-making related to pricing must be accelerated by a factor of ten. Moreover, a relentless focus on continuous implementation and performance tracking is essential. The role of the control tower also encompasses validating pricing strategies with a high likelihood of success through pilot testing and swiftly adapting them based on results.

Lotte Mart serves as an exemplar in this regard. Since

2022, the company has operated a dedicated "pricing team" under the direct leadership of its CEO. This specialized team employs a meticulous analysis of product characteristics to manage prices intensively, making real-time adjustments and exploring alternative solutions when needed. For instance, when anticipating an increase in pork belly prices, Lotte Mart rapidly triples its imports of pork belly to ensure a competitive and reasonable price point for consumers.

It is crucial to recognize that the variable pricing strategy has both positive and negative aspects. On the one hand, implementing various prices can enhance a company's profitability. However, it can also have the unintended consequence of diminishing customers' consumer surplus. "Consumer surplus" refers to the benefit that consumers derive when they purchase a product at a price lower than what they were willing to pay. As pricing becomes more segmented, consumer surplus tends to decrease while corporate profits rise. Consequently, the key to the success or failure of variable pricing strategies lies in how they are designed to positively impact both consumer welfare and business outcomes.

Aligning with consumer values

To execute a successful variable pricing strategy, especially for consumers who are highly sensitive to even minor price differences, it's essential to ensure that price discrimination is acceptable to consumers. Sarah Maxwell, the author of *The Price is Wrong: Understanding What Makes a Price Seem Fair and the True Cost of Unfair Pricing*, emphasizes the importance of a fair price recognized by consumers, one that satisfies both personal and societal notions of fairness. From a personal perspective, a fair price is one that aligns with individual expectations and affordability, while from a societal viewpoint, it's a price perceived as equitable for all.

Consumers who are exposed to extremely low prices due to flexible pricing policies often come to expect such prices or even take them for granted, assuming they will receive regular coupons or discount vouchers. Ultra-low prices have become the new norm and are perceived as fair. In such cases, it becomes challenging to establish a fair price point in the future, and every price change is met with skepticism, raising questions like, "Is this a fair price?" Research on the frequency and scarcity of discounts suggests that consumers tend to perceive the reference price of products offered by companies with frequent discounts as lower. Furthermore, excessive price fluctuations can impact customers' perceptions of a brand and their expectations, potentially causing doubts about the brand's consistency and reliability.

While AI can offer convenience, it also has the potential to neutralize one of consumers' most potent tools: price comparison. If AI sets prices based on variables like income, gender, age, or race, it could lead to significant social and ethical concerns. A notable historical example is the discovery in 2000 that Amazon was raising prices for loyal customers while lowering prices for those with no purchase history, which sparked a boycott and an apology from CEO Jeff Bezos.

However, the phenomenon of various pricing strategies operating within the boundaries of social norms and ethics is a characteristic trend in the modern economy. Price differentiation serves not only as a means to maximize profits for producers and distributors but also as an opportunity to establish a variable pricing strategy that balances corporate growth and consumer welfare by offering prices deemed acceptable to consumers. The paramount consideration is that prices should unequivocally reflect the value perceived by the customer.

Professor Emeritus Yoon Seok-cheol윤석철 of Seoul National University's College of Business introduced the requisite formula for "survival inequality that creates a great company" as follows:

Cost of product < Price of product < Value of product

Indeed, it's crucial to remember that when the price of a product falls short of the value perceived by customers, sustaining the company's long-term viability becomes a challenge.

On
Dopamine Farming

As the phrase "Homo ludens" (man at play) implies, humans are fun-seekers. While the desire to play is nothing new, there's something unique about the way we do it nowadays that has never been seen before. We'll call it "dopamine farming": the effort to try and collect anything that will give you a dopamine rush that can bring you pleasure.

Dopamine farming behaviors vary. Here are four types of dopaminergic behaviors: First, there's the fun of randomness. To experience the thrill of serendipity, people deliberately push themselves into moments where the outcome is unpredictable. Second, there's the fun of deviation, which is experienced in outlandish situations that go against the grain. This includes the euphoria and release that comes from doing something out of the ordinary and over the top. Third, we experience fun in reckless pursuits where the challenge itself is pointless and the outcome is unknown. It's the thrill of being in a situation that makes your hands sweat and gives you a tremendous sense of urgency and accomplishment. Finally, we enjoy the bizarre and seemingly sadistic pleasure of self-inflicted stress and the welcome pleasure that comes with its release. One person's stressful behavior is another's refreshing fun.

Dopamine makes us feel happy, but it's only released in response to new stimuli, so we seek out more and more stimulating pleasures over time. This is where serotonin comes in. Serotonin is the hormone that is released when you are relaxed, meditating, and helping others. If dopamine is the accelerator, serotonin is the brake. A car without an accelerator won't move, but a car without brakes will crash. They need to be in harmony. To achieve true happiness, you need to balance your dopamine-driven life with your serotonin-driven life.

A man constructed a 1,360kg concrete coffin to bury a bag of Cheetos. This unusual project took place in November 2022, courtesy of "Sunday Nobody Art," a self-proclaimed "meme artist" who documented the five-month-long endeavor on his TikTok account. Surprisingly, his videos garnered nearly 10 million views within just two days. When asked, "Why do you do this?" his response was simple: "Because it's fun."

There exist individuals who engage in activities purely for the sake of enjoyment. A growing number of people partake in such pursuits, sharing them with others, devoid of significant meaning or financial gain. Humans are inherently Homo ludens, creatures designed for play. Our innate drive leads us to seek enjoyment and recreation.

The desire for play has always been a part of human nature, but there's something distinctly modern about the way people pursue fun today. The most significant shift is the incredible diversity and brevity of what people find enjoyable. Notably, platforms like TikTok, with its incredibly successful 15-second format, as well as Instagram Reels and YouTube Shorts, have embraced the trend of releasing short and engaging content.

YouTube, for instance, introduced Shorts in 2020, featuring videos of one minute or less. According to Collab Asia, a global creator agency, as of January 2023, more than 80% of YouTube's viewer engagement stems from Shorts. We now inhabit a world where easily accessible, quick bursts of stimulating fun are always at our fingertips.

The neurotransmitter that floods our system when we encounter something novel and enjoyable is known as dopamine. While it's a fact that humans are naturally drawn to pleasure, contemporary society takes this pursuit to a new level. Today, people are unwilling to tolerate even a moment of boredom; they yearn for a perpetual state of dopamine release. In this book, we will dub this phenomenon "dopamine farming," as individuals actively seek amusement across a broad spectrum of activities and are averse to its absence. In gaming terminology, "farming" refers to players collecting items to enhance their in-game characters' abilities, akin to cultivating crops. Thus, dopamine farming symbolizes the quest for diverse experiences that trigger dopamine rushes and deliver gratification.

A "dopamine high"도파민 돈다 (or "dopamine rush," "dopamine runs") is a common expression among young people these days. It's a way of saying that something is fun, super interesting, or that it simply makes you feel good. It also often appears in entertainment headlines. "Dopamine rush! '*Swoo-pa* (*Street Woman Fighter*) 2' is crazy from the first episode," "Dopamine at its finest! '*I Am Solo*' season 16, rising above controversy and malice," "Dopamine King: '*Mask Girl*' rises to global top 2 in 3 days," and so on. "Dopamine" is used to express the fact that a program is fun and well-received. Recently, young people have also been taking "dopamine addiction tests," which are not serious medical tests, but just fun online tests to share with friends to say, for example, "I'm 1,000,000% dopamine addicted." This trend reflects the perspective of a younger generation that regards dopamine as a source of amusement.

Four Types of Dopamine Farming

1. Random situation dopamine farming

"What do you think I should wear to work today?"

Recently, "random outfits" have been trending on social media. The #RandomCoordinationChallenge랜덤코디챌린지, in which even the participants themselves do not know what they will wear that day, is giving people an unexpected dopamine rush. The protagonist of this challenge is blindfolded and has to choose between two options placed on their right and left sides. From top to bottom, accessories to shoes, the final outfit is created by randomly selecting one of the two views. Sometimes the result is a great outfit, but more often than not, it's a hodgepodge of mismatched clothes that make viewers laugh. Even the editors of *Cosmopolitan Korea*, a fashion magazine that provides readers with stylish outfit suggestions, have joined in on the random outfit challenge, posting their wacky outfits on Instagram.

This represents the first category of dopamine farming, namely, the enjoyment derived from the unpredictability of outcomes. Just as unexpected surprises are more thrilling, people find excitement in situations where the outcome remains uncertain. According to psychiatrist Lee Sung-chan이성찬, the human brain has an inherent preference for unpredictable events over predictable ones. Scientists refer to this phenomenon as "reward prediction error." The concept revolves around the idea that our brains perpetually function like radar, attempting to anticipate future events, and when the actual outcome significantly deviates from our predictions, we experience a heightened sense of satisfaction, accompanied by the release of dopamine.

Even in the food and beverage industry, where consumer preferences hold significant sway, randomness can introduce an element of surprise and delight. In certain Starbucks drive-throughs across the United States, the concept of "ran-

domized drink ordering" adds a playful twist to the experience. Instead of specifying a particular beverage, customers
simply request the barista to: "make it your favorite." The
thrill lies in the uncertainty of what you'll receive.

As you eagerly approach the pickup point, the barista
serves you their personal favorite drink. While it's perfectly
acceptable to suggest a moderately popular beverage, the
staff genuinely enjoy recommending their personal favor-
ites. Occasionally, friendly debates arise between staff and
customers regarding their drink of choice. Importantly,
customers are never displeased with the surprise drink they
receive, relishing the opportunity to try something outside
of their usual choices.

In Korea, there are some shops that sell alcoholic bev-
erages that are completely unpredictable. Located near
Seongsu Station in Seoul, Mugeunbon무근본, meaning "unrooted"
is a self-described "non-specialty store" that sells soju,
beer, whisky, cocktails, and more, and is witty in its lack
of roots in everything from its interior to its menu. The
table at which customers drink is a glass display case for
smartphones that used to be a roadside stand for a telecoms
company. The shop's signature drink is called the "gaessup
unrooted cocktail개쌉무근본칵테일," which is mostly meaning-
less and is whatever drink the bartender wants to serve to
customers. Furthermore, some of the snacks are creatively
named, like "I'm practicing by watching YouTube유튜브 보고 연

습중인 것," and "Hey, what is this? It's so yummy야이거 뭔데 맛있냐" The enjoyable aspect lies in the fact that these names provide no clear indication of what the item will taste like, keeping customers in suspense until they take their first bite or sip.

2. Dopamine farming the unexpected and outlandish

In August 2023, a very unusual DJ party was held in Yeo-uido Hangang Park. Music festivals are typically known for their deafening noise, but at this particular DJ party, an unusual hush prevailed. Around 300 enthusiastic attendees donned blue-light headphones and danced fervently in absolute silence, creating a surreal spectacle. For passersby, witnessing festival-goers passionately reveling in the absence of audible music at this "silent disco" might have seemed peculiar. However, thanks to an unconventional plan that defied common sense, this extraordinary and entertaining "Noiseless DJ Festival" managed to capture the attention of the public. Notably, it earned positive reviews from local residents who had long endured the disruptive noise of existing festivals.

This represents the second category of dopamine farming: enjoyment derived from engaging in activities that deviate from the ordinary and routine, even if they may appear strange to others. People often find a unique sense of liberation and delight in stepping outside the norm.

In recent times, companies have also embraced unconventional forms of entertainment. Take the "Super Race Championship," sponsored by CJ Logistics, for instance. This event has been Korea's premier motorsports competition since 2006. Traditionally, the competition features high-end supercars with hefty price tags and top-notch specifications, all striving to shave off a mere 0.001 seconds from their lap times. Spectators, in turn, find themselves on the edge of their seats, engrossed in the intensity of the race.

However, in August 2023, it was the pre-ceremony event that stole the spotlight before the actual race even began. Instead of the usual high-performance supercars, eight ordinary blue delivery trucks commonly seen on the streets took to the speedway circuit. The audience erupted in shouts and cheers, fully engaged in the exhilarating race between these unlikely contenders. This unconventional marketing approach, straying far from the norm, turned out to be unexpectedly impactful and generated significant buzz.

3. Dopamine farming through reckless challenges

The third category of dopamine farming is characterized by the enjoyment derived from pursuing audacious goals where success is uncertain. This form of enjoyment encompasses two distinct aspects. Firstly, the challenge itself is often deemed reckless to such an extent that observers may question why anyone would undertake it. Secondly, the excitement arises not only from the challenge but also from witnessing the uncertain journey toward success. When a challenger teeters on the brink of success, the audience is engulfed in a thrilling sense of anticipation and pleasure.

The energy drink giant Red Bull stands as a prime example of a company that has achieved success through daring marketing strategies designed to trigger a full release of dopamine. In 2007, Red Bull established its subsidiary "Red Bull Media House," which actively supports ambitious projects that push the limits of human capabilities. A notable endeavor was "Red Bull Stratos" in 2012, where Austrian skydiver Felix Baumgartner donned a spacesuit and free fell from a staggering 39 kilometers above Earth, hurtling at speeds of 1,357 kilometers per hour. This historic supersonic descent, humanity's first, captivated the attention of 8 million viewers, marking the largest audience for a YouTube live broadcast at the time.

Red Bull's successful completion of this audacious challenge was estimated to have generated an advertising impact of approximately $40 billion at that time, bolstering its positive image as a staunch supporter of athletes driven by boundless passion. Thanks to such endeavors, Red Bull is renowned as "a media company, not a beverage company," and has adopted the concept of "storydoing" in its marketing, a step beyond mere storytelling. In September 2023, the inaugural "Red Bull Cliff Diving World Series" took place in Korea, hosted in collaboration with the Seoul Metropolitan

Government and the Seoul Tourism Foundation, further cementing the company's reputation for bold and thrilling initiatives.

In addition to excitement-seeking brands, there exists a community of individuals who derive enjoyment from a multitude of daring challenges. One such endeavor is this intriguing challenge: "Go from Seoul to Busan by city bus in 24 hours." This event, originating from a city bus enthusiasts' club, presents a formidable challenge: embarking from Seoul and reaching Busan within the tight timeframe of 24 hours. To successfully complete this race, participants must strictly adhere to a pre-determined route without any deviations.

Most challengers set out on their journey around midnight, usually from Gangnam Station or Seoul Station. During layovers, they might catch a brief nap in a PC room, or they may have to sprint long distances to catch the next express bus. Despite the relative convenience of public transportation and good road infrastructure in Korea, as the journey progresses, time becomes an increasingly precious commodity. While many challengers inevitably fall short of the mark, those who manage to cross the finish line with a mere two minutes to spare before midnight, along with those who follow their adventures through videos, collectively breathe a sigh of relief.

The spectacle of individuals relishing in the excitement of

taking on audacious challenges often serves as a prominent theme in online video content. A prime example of this can be found in the exploits of comedian Jeong Jae-hyung, a member of the popular YouTube channel "Psick Univ피식대학." Beginning in 2020, on the day of the CSAT (College Scholastic Ability Test) in Korea, he embarked on a "CSAT Cheer Live Broadcast," lasting for approximately seven hours through the duration of the test.

At first glance, there may not be anything particularly extraordinary about cheering on college entrance test-takers. All one typically has to do is sit quietly in front of the screen, mimicking the role of an actual exam proctor. However, what sets this challenge apart is that viewers intentionally leave humorous comments aimed at disrupting Jeong Jae-hyung's composure. Yet, the sight of him valiantly suppressing laughter and fatigue while maintaining his upright position during the extended broadcast adds a unique layer of enjoyment. It creates an experience akin to that of a genuine exam proctor, while offering viewers a dose of amusement.

4. Dopamine farming after bizarre and sadistic stress

The last type of dopamine farming involves discovering unexpected enjoyment in peculiar experiences that evoke pain and fear. People intentionally visit haunted houses at amusement parks, where they shudder in fear and scream to their heart's content, only to exclaim afterward, "That was fun!" Similarly, even after watching a gruesome and spine-chilling horror movie, the sensation of relief from the tension is often described as fun. In these instances, the thrill of encountering fear and overcoming it adds a unique dimension to the pleasure derived from such unconventional and unsettling experiences. As Professor Yoon Dae-hyun of the Department of Psychiatry at Seoul National University Hospital explains, "Dopamine is released when we see something pleasing and beautiful, but it's also released when we see something scary, crazy, and frightening."

Among the videos people enjoy watching, there is a genre called "ASMR(Autonomous Sensory Meridian Response)." ASMR is a form of psychological relaxation, sometimes associated with a tingling sensation, that can come from visual or auditory stimuli such as wind blowing, a pencil writing, or paper rustling. However, recently, a new concept video is emerging that breaks the stereotype that ASMR videos must be calming videos. This is a case of using bizarre material such as sebum extraction, fine hair removal, acne extrusion, and tartar removal as the subject of the video. ASMR specialist YouTube channel "Smile Bam스마일밤," which has 4.13 million subscribers as of September 2023, produces videos with the hashtag #OSV – Oddly Satisfying Video. Among them, the tonsil stones (tonsilloliths) treatment video has racked up 25 million views as of September 2023.

Some individuals derive enjoyment from participating in extreme and seemingly sadistic physical activities. A relatively recent phenomenon known as "slap fighting" has gained popularity worldwide, originating in Russia. The first slap fight event took place in 2019 on the sidelines of the "Siberian Power Show," with a video featuring Vasily Kamotsky, a farmer, going viral on YouTube. The enthusiasm for slap fighting extended to the United States, where even the world's largest mixed martial arts organization, the UFC, introduced its own version called "Power Slap."

In a surprising turn of events, the Nevada State Athletic Commission officially licensed slap fighting as an official sport in 2022. In 2023, the American cable channel TBS even produced a reality TV show centered around power slaps. The sheer force exerted by the athletes' hands in these contests can be likened to being struck by a small truck, and viewers often experience a strange mix of fascination and discomfort – a guilty pleasure – while watching this brutal competition unfold.

A growing number of people are discovering that stress can provide them with a dopamine rush. This phenomenon is particularly evident in popular music genres like rap, hip-hop, and dance, which share a common element: the "diss." Diss culture revolves around mocking and taunting opponents, often by exposing their weaknesses and accusing them of all manner of wrongdoing. Dissing (short for "disrespecting") encapsulates the act of dismantling an adversary's spirit through verbal attacks.

One of the notable introductions of diss culture to Korean society was through the rap and hip-hop talent show, 'Show Me the Money.' On this show, participating rappers engage in diss battles디스전, during which they target their opponents' vulnerabilities, frequently employing offensive lyrics. The sight of rappers swearing and engaging in verbal duels on television creates significant psychological tension. Swearing is typically considered taboo in social settings, and when it occurs, it can generate a strong sense of tension and discomfort. However, as soon as the confrontation is over, there's a sudden release of that tension, leading to a feeling of relief that viewers often describe as "refreshing시원하다," like a form of catharsis.

Why We Are Drawn to Dopamine Farming

Dopamine farming addicts enjoy the unexpected in random situations. They take pleasure in deviating from the norm by acting outlandishly or exaggerating reality. They enjoy reckless challenges that don't mean much to them and find a sense of accomplishment and release from sadistic stress. Why is it that people are so into absurd fun these days?

People are increasingly drawn to dopamine farming for

several reasons. Firstly, there has been a shift in societal attitudes towards the concept of "fun." In the past, especially in societies with strong Confucian traditions like Korea, fun was often viewed as a frivolous pursuit. It was seen as a mere diversion from productive work, with work and one's occupation being prioritized as the primary endeavors. Fun was essentially relegated to a way of unwinding during one's free time.

However, in the modern world the boundaries between work and play have become less distinct. The era of rigidly separating work and leisure is giving way to a more integrated approach, where playfulness has found its way into the workplace. There's a growing recognition of the value of play as a means of rejuvenation amidst the daily grind. People are starting to appreciate that fun can provide them with a sense of vitality through the tension and relaxation it offers.

What was once considered a secondary pursuit has now evolved into a life goal and a vital aspect that enhances our overall quality of life. The desire for enjoyable and unconventional experiences, such as dopamine farming, reflects this evolving perspective on fun as an essential attribute that enriches our lives.

It's essential to acknowledge that the evolution of how people have fun is closely intertwined with changes in the media they use. Professor Kim Seon-jin김선진, from Kyungsung University's Department of Media Studies, emphasizes in his book, *The Essence of Fun*재미의 본질, that shifts in communication methods also usher in changes in thinking patterns and cultural characteristics that dominate each era.

The world of written language, where thoughts are conveyed through letters, has developed into the world of video language, where thoughts are conveyed through media. During the era of written language, the essence of fun often resided subtly within the nuances of words and sentences, rather than being immediately apparent. However, in the world of visual language characterized by instant communication, the demand for fun is swifter and more direct.

In this landscape, all forms of content must be engaging, regardless of their subject matter, as the audience's interests can swiftly shift to other channels or platforms. This trend is particularly pronounced with the emergence of short-form content on various social media platforms, like YouTube Shorts and Instagram Reels. With consumers' attention spans progressively shortening, the type of entertainment people seek has evolved to become more visual, visceral, intuitive, and intense compared to the past. In this fast-paced and visually driven environment, fun must captivate quickly and hold attention effectively.

More fundamentally, it can be seen as a reaction to the performance-driven mindset that has intensified since the COVID-19 pandemic. In dopamine farming, the key word is "just그냥," reflecting the younger generation's values of living life in a carefree manner. It represents a deviation towards fun in response to the societal pressure to lead a serious and demanding life.

Outlook & Implications

Industrial response

In December 2022, convenience store chain CU held the "CU Concert," the industry's first "Convenience Store Special Comedian'" selection contest. The final winner of the survival program receives a prize of 10 million won and is hired as a special comedian by BGF Retail, the operator of CU, to host various in-house events. Another convenience store company, GS25, is also strengthening comedy content on its official YouTube channel. In July 2022, they hit 1 million subscribers and received their Gold Play Button Creator Award.

The emphasis on fun in the convenience store channel, despite its primary focus on providing convenience, can be attributed to the evolving competitive landscape in the business world. As products and services become increasingly standardized, companies find themselves in a situation where they must continuously compete not only with other industry players but also with individual nano-influencers, who have the power to sway consumer choices. In such a scenario, fun emerges as a standout attribute that can genuinely capture the hearts of consumers. It's a universal desire to be associated with those who bring laughter and joy into our lives.

To leverage the burgeoning trend of dopamine farming and truly resonate with consumers, companies must infuse every facet of their operations with engaging and enjoyable elements. For example, Lotte Mart released the song 'Watermelon Song수박송' in collaboration with the indie band 'Kakimajem카키마젬' in June 2023. Rather than conveying the high sugar content of watermelon through numbers, it is expressed through witty song lyrics. 'Watermelon Song' exceeded 10,000 views in just two days after it was released on Lotte Mart's official social media account, with consumers commenting: "I'm going to buy a watermelon right now," and "It's a song that makes me want to eat watermelon." It's the fun factor that draws consumers.

In the future, companies will need to go beyond merely offering fun to consumers and actively engage them by suggesting ways to participate in enjoyable activities. Ty Montague, founder of brand marketing company "co:collective," proposed the concept of "storydoing." As was the case with Red Bull's Stratos "Space Jump," where the brand went beyond energy drinks to challenge human limits, storydoing is a way to go one step further from "storytelling" and put a brand's story into action for maximum engagement.

Life in harmony

Indeed, fun is of great importance. As the famous American proverb goes, "All work and no play makes Jack a dull boy." However, our pursuit of happiness and enjoyment is not solely reliant on dopamine. Happy and pleasurable emotions are connected to two key neurotransmitters: dopamine and serotonin.

Dopamine is a neurotransmitter closely linked to exhilarating fun. It is released when we encounter unexpected good fortune, such as winning a competition or a lottery. The secretion of dopamine can increase motivation and excitement for work. However, its effects are short-lived, and people can quickly build tolerance, leading to a desire for stronger and more intense stimulation. This is why dopamine has earned the less favorable nickname: the "addiction hormone."

On the other hand, serotonin is a neurotransmitter associated with small and simple pleasures. It is released when engaging in activities like taking a walk, meditating, or looking at cute pictures of animals. Serotonin is connected to actions that remain enjoyable no matter how many times they are repeated. Due to this characteristic, it has earned the nickname: the "happiness hormone."

As we've observed, there are growing concerns that our society is gradually shifting toward one dominated by the short-lived and highly stimulating effects of dopamine. The dopamine farming trend, which places a premium on fun, should not be seen as advocating for dopamine to overpower serotonin. To draw an analogy, consider dopamine as the accelerator and serotonin as the brake in a car. A car without an accelerator won't move, but a car without brakes can lead to accidents. What's essential is a balance between the two.

Dopamine is crucial for living with excitement in every moment, while serotonin plays a vital role in enduring life with a steady, long-term perspective. Achieving a harmonious blend of these neurotransmitters is necessary for a well-rounded and fulfilling life.

To attain genuine happiness, it's essential to strike a balance between the dopamine-driven and serotonin-driven aspects of life. We should aim to engage in enjoyable activities more frequently, savor them fully, and sustain a state of ongoing happiness in our lives.

Not Like Old Daddies, Millennial Hubbies

The values of family life and gender roles have changed dramatically in recent years. With the age of marriage getting higher and higher and the lifetime unmarried rate soaring, "millennial husbands요즘남편," who choose to enter the difficult path of marriage, and "new (heretofore unseen) dads없던아빠," with a parenting mindset that is unfamiliar to older generations, are emerging.

First of all, the road to marriage has become long and difficult. After the big proposal and the wedding ceremony, the division of household finances and domestic work becomes a major issue in newlywed life. As dual-income families have become commonplace and the division of household labor has become natural, wives are ready to take over the role of head of the household and provide support if their income is high. It is important for husbands to share household chores with an active attitude of "doing my job as a matter of course" rather than one of "just helping out." Once you have a child, your role as a father expands. Fathers study parenting books, choose their own baby products, and become "6 o'clock Cinderellas" who go straight home from work to spend time with their children. There is a paradox in this trend. These changes are putting pressure on the decision to get married. Women are entering the workforce and men are entering the home, and even after marriage, both wives and husbands are becoming multitaskers, juggling work and family. As a result, marriage, childbirth, and childcare are becoming more demanding, and many people are giving up on marriage and childbirth altogether. In order to solve the problem of the declining birthrate, it is time to consider support measures for fathers, who bear half the responsibility. Will these new dads be the last hope to revive Korea's dwindling marriage and birth rate?

"My married life can feel like work. It requires the same dedication as I have with a job or a lifelong career. Just because this is my marital abode doesn't mean I should behave as if I live in solitude. Undoubtedly, this is my chosen path, and I believe in doing my best here to weave together various stories. So, I aspire for my married life to be an enjoyable journey."

Renowned hip-hop artist Beenzino shared his perspective on marriage during a recent interview, sparking a viral discussion on social media platforms. He said that he thought of married life as a vocation, not in the sense of "I must do it, reluctantly," but rather as a career that demands one's utmost dedication. As one of Korea's most prominent rappers, he insists that his eight-year relationship-turned-marriage is also a job demanding his best effort. Marriage tends to naturally evolve as one ages, and for men who once prioritized work over family life, this notion may appear quite unfamiliar.

Ideas surrounding marriage and family dynamics are undergoing a significant transformation, particularly in terms of evolving perspectives among men. The descriptors used to portray men in the media have similarly evolved. Instead of the conventional and stern concept of "the head of the family," we now encounter more affable and progressive terms like "the king of domestic support내조왕," signifying a man who actively supports his wife's career pursuits, and "the household manager살림남," for a man who exhibits his own proficiency in domestic affairs. The term "doting father딸·아들바보," has also become common.

This isn't just some story on the silver screen. The role of the household leader isn't set in stone, but adaptable to different circumstances. There are men challenging the conventional idea that men should fit a certain mold. Just as women, raised as beloved daughters, pursue education and careers, they too understand that men must not only work but also fulfill multifaceted roles as husbands, fathers, sons, and sons-in-law. This context gives rise to the emergence of "millennial husbands," who grapple with the demanding reality of balancing work and childcare responsibilities.

These changes can also be understood by looking at the results of a social survey conducted by Statistics Korea. Compared to 2015, in 2021, responses across society saying "I prioritize work" decreased and responses saying "I prioritize family life" increased. In particular, men in their 30s showed the most dramatic change from 11.7% to 23.7%.

However, we currently inhabit an era where only one

in three (36.4%) young individuals express optimism about marriage. Notably, the values concerning family life and gender roles among millennials in their 30s and early 40s are undergoing substantial transformations. With the average age of marriage rising and the lifelong unmarried rate surging, a new wave of husbands who have consciously embarked on the challenging journey of matrimony, and fathers who embrace child-rearing with a mindset quite distinct from older generations, is emerging in growing numbers.

Living as a Millennial Husband

"Nowadays, appearance takes the lead as the first criterion, followed by economic stability. This change is underscored by the fact that women's social status and capabilities are on the rise. Some women even assert, 'I am capable of earning and supporting my partner.'"

– from an interview with a manager of a matchmaking company

The traditional belief that economic power matters most for men, while appearance is crucial for women, is eroding in the context of spouse selection. During an interview with the Consumer Trend Insights team, a manager from 'Duo듀오', a matchmaking company boasting the largest membership in Korea for over two decades, offered the foregoing response when asked about the kind of men preferred by today's brides. As women's financial independence grows, they now also attach importance to a man's physical appearance.

Furthermore, the process of finding a partner has evolved. It is no longer unusual for a woman to propose a follow-up meeting after the initial encounter, or assert that, having purchased her own home, all she requires is a marriage partner. In essence, the roles and appearances expected of men in the context of spouse selection are experiencing a transformation.

The long and winding road to marriage: Taking the first step

While physical appearance often takes the top spot in initial impressions, the genuine qualities sought in a spouse revolve around financial stability. Economic power encompasses not just income and assets but also a secure job and family circumstances, including parental retirement funds, which can involve pensions or monthly rental revenue from real estate.

Lifestyle compatibility is another crucial facet. Marriage and parenthood now stem from personal values rather than societal expectations, making it essential to discuss not only the intention to marry but also the timing of marriage and plans for children before taking the plunge. Couples must weigh whether they envision a married life filled with shared hobbies or aspire to be a "FIRE tribe" member, achieving financial independence and retiring early, as well as saving and investing diligently. Cultural compatibility is equally vital. Factors like the number of siblings one has and family traditions, such as observing ancestral rites on holidays, are subjects of inquiry.

Indeed, selecting a bride poses its own set of challenges. While appearance continues to hold significance, there's a growing recognition that relying solely on men to accumulate wealth through economic pursuits is increasingly demanding. Consequently, women's job stability and economic independence have gained importance in the spouse selection process.

According to insights from a Duo's manager, the quest for a life partner is becoming progressively intricate to the extent that some men may favor an only daughter over a second daughter. As the desire to find the perfect match intensifies, it has led to a surge not only among twenty to thirty-somethings seeking the services of matchmaking companies, but also in the proliferation of diverse matchmaking options. These encompass everything from overnight activity-based matchmaking events to dating apps that require employment verification before joining, reflecting the evolving landscape of modern courtship.

Once you've found your life partner, you embark on the extensive journey of preparing for marriage. Among the challenges, setting up a new home stands out as one of the most daunting tasks. Given the increasing difficulty for ordinary office workers to single-handedly purchase a home, the traditional notion of "Men buy houses; women buy household items" has become a relic of the past.

In its place, the concept of "half-half marriages" has emerged, where both the bride and groom contribute equally to cover housing expenses. According to a survey conducted by Duo, among newlyweds who tied the knot within the past two years, men typically bear around 60% (172.72 million won) of the marriage expenses, with women covering the remaining 40% (114.67 million won). Notably, a significant 84% of the total wedding expenditures are allocated toward establishing the newlywed's home.

As the idea of couples collaboratively pooling their resources gains traction, respondents in the survey expressed a preference for channeling their finances into meaningful investments such as household items or a honeymoon, rather than adhering to traditional practices that entail substantial wedding presents to the spouse's family.

Dividing millennial husband roles: Starting today, I am the housekeeper

The title of a widely viewed YouTube video, boasting 9.84 million views (as of September 2023), reads, "If my wife earns 1 billion won a year, I can do this." In the video, the moment the husband receives a text message from his wife that she's coming home, he springs into action. He promptly rushes to the door to welcome her, takes her bag, escorts her inside, and meticulously ensures her comfort by handling tasks such as opening and closing doors, including the refrigerator and microwave. His thoughtfulness aims to take care of every conceivable need. The video's comments section is filled with accolades for the wife, with statements like, "An annual salary of 1 billion won! Just by walking on her own feet, she's an angel."

In the context of contemporary husbands, traditional patriarchy has evolved into a historical relic. In the capitalist households of millennials, the role of the household's leader is now defined by economic prowess rather than gender. The conventional stereotype dictating that men are responsible for economic endeavors while women handle household chores is undergoing a significant transformation, giving rise to a more diversified and dynamic family dynamic.

In the case of dual-income households, there's a growing consensus that it's a reasonable choice for the husband to take parental leave, especially if the wife's income is higher. This shift is not just in perception but also evident in statistical data. According to January 2023 data from Statistics Korea, there are 215,000 men who are not participating in economic activities due to their involvement in housework. This marks the highest figure in two decades since January

2003, highlighting a gradual long-term increase in the number of men taking on full responsibility for household chores. Additionally, there are 17,000 men who are economically inactive due to childcare, the highest number recorded since statistics began tracking in 1999.

While the proportion of men who are not economically active and are taking full responsibility of housework and childcare is still relatively small compared to women, standing at approximately 1/30, it represents a noteworthy trend. This trend signifies that while the number of those economically inactive due to childcare is decreasing among men, the number of men actively engaged in childcare responsibilities is on the rise.

The emergence of new (heretofore unseen) fathers

- *Waiting at the apartment complex for the kindergarten bus*
- *Weekend pediatric appointments*
- *Weekend outings to the department store culture center*
- *Weekend visits to the playground*

What ties these places together? They are where you'll encounter dads who, due to their weekday work commitments, make a special effort to spend quality time with their children. These fathers dutifully accompany their children to kindergarten or school in the early mornings and care for them during weekends, whether at hospitals, department stores, cultural centers, or playgrounds. The traditional scene of a mother and child waving goodbye to the father leaving for work in the early morning has undergone a profound transformation. These days, it's the fathers who drop off their children at kindergarten on their way to work. Parenthood is no longer solely the mother's domain; it's a shared responsibility among parents, and fathers are being reborn as "new (heretofore unseen) fathers" - a nonexistent role in previous generations.

Changes in fathers' roles are exerting a notable influence on the workplace, marked by a rising trend of fathers opting for parental leave. According to recent data from Statistics Korea, in 2021 there were 173,631 individuals who availed parental leave for children under the age of eight (the second grade of elementary school), with 24.1% of them being men. This marks the first time that men constituted more than 20% of those taking parental leave, representing a 1.5% increase in just one year. While it is somewhat disheartening that over 70% of male paternity leave takers are employed by large corporations, this trend is nevertheless a positive step forward.

Equipment-friendly fathers: More enjoyable housework
As fathers become more involved in household chores and childcare, their contributions are shaping the family

landscape in new ways. One example is their adoption of smart home technology and AI speakers for various tasks. Beyond traditional appliances like dishwashers, dryers, and robot vacuum cleaners, these modern households are equipped with IoT-controlled electrical switches, enabling the realization of a truly smart home environment. Men who take a keen interest in operating electronic devices find that this technology significantly enhances the efficiency of housework, transforming once tedious tasks into enjoyable and engaging activities.

The influence of men extends not only to the large home appliance market but also to the realm of small home appliances. For instance, during a home shopping broadcast selling Dyson vacuum cleaners, viewership ratings among men in their 20s and 30s were twice as high as those among women of the same age group. Moreover, in LG Electronics' "Code Zero A9" experience group, men accounted for a substantial 45%, indicating significant interest in the high-performance cordless vacuum cleaner market.

Recently, food waste disposers have gained popularity as a home appliance. GS Home Shopping reported that after TVs and vacuum cleaners, food waste disposers emerged as the next most-purchased home appliance by male buyers. Furthermore, an analysis of sales data for the first quarter of 2023 by gender and age conducted by "Most X모스트엑스," a food waste disposer manufacturer, revealed that men in their

40s constituted the largest proportion of all buyers, surpassing women in this particular market.

Complexity of the 'Decision to Marry'

This shift represents a "predestined future" brought about by the entrance of women into the workforce, leading to a transformation in gender roles and responsibilities. According to 2022 data, the economic activity participation rate in Korea stands at 73.5% for men and 54.6% for women. Over the past two decades, the number of men in the workforce has decreased, while the number of women has increased. Consequently, the gender gap has significantly narrowed from 25.6% in 2000 to 18.9% in 2023.

Furthermore, the prevalence of dual-income households has been on the rise, accounting for 46.1% of all households. Among households in their 30s, the age group embarking on new family life, the dual-income ratio is even higher at 54.2%, surpassing the halfway mark as of the second half of 2022.

Economist and Harvard University professor Claudia Goldin conceptualizes this societal transformation as "a grand gender convergence." This term signifies that while complete gender equality has not yet been attained, the lives of men and women, once characterized by distinct domains such as work, housework, and childcare, have converged into a shared sphere. In many aspects, including roles, opportunities, and experiences, the lives of men and women have grown increasingly similar, symbolizing a significant shift in societal dynamics.

The changing trends described so far can indeed impose a significant burden on young men considering marriage. This is because the concept of masculinity that millennial men have grown up with differs substantially from that of their fathers' generation, making this transition challenging. For women who desire marriage, it's also a formidable task to commit to marriage unless their potential spouse embraces this evolving mindset. Notably, the number of marriages in South Korea has been steadily declining year after year. According to data from Statistics Korea, the number of new marriages, which stood at 323,000 in 2013, dropped by nearly 40% to 192,000 in 2022, in less than a decade. Even when accounting for the declining youth population, this decline is happening at an accelerated pace. Each time birth rate statistics are released, they reflect an all-time low. In 2022, Korea's birth rate was 0.78, and the birth rate in the first half of 2023 appears to have decreased compared to the same period the previous year, painting a bleak picture. Furthermore, over half (53.5%) of young respondents aged 19 to 34 have expressed the belief that "there is no need to have children even if you get married," indicating that even becoming a father within a marriage is increasingly challenging in today's context.

There are several analyses regarding the declining rates of marriage and childbirth. The first reason cited is the substantial economic barriers, including marriage costs and housing affordability. However, there's another contemporary factor contributing to this phenomenon. According to Northwestern University Professor Eli Finkel, who specializes in social psychology of marriage, modern society sees marriage as an "all-or-nothing" decision – a choice that can lead to either extreme happiness or deep unhappiness.

Marriage has evolved from a societal obligation to an individual's subjective choice. Today, it requires extensive and diverse considerations. Besides establishing a stable home, it necessitates the fundamental condition of mutual romantic love. Additionally, the relationship should foster mutual support and encourage each partner's self-realization, rather than merely demanding sacrifice for the family. Professor Finkel draws a parallel with Maslow's hierarchy of needs: just as satisfying survival needs leads to safety, and subsequently to belonging, esteem, and self-actualization, individuals increasingly seek higher-level needs in marriage. Consequently, achieving one's desired outcomes through marriage has become more challenging, demanding significant time and effort. This is why being a married couple today is more demanding than ever.

Moreover, there's an issue of asymmetrical gender convergence between men and women. While women increasingly engage in professional activities, becoming more independent and empowered, men's acceptance of femininity lags. This discrepancy is closely linked to the persistent problem of household inequality that continues to be a topic of concern. According to the Statistics Korea 2022 report, only around 20% of both husbands and wives reported that they shared household responsibilities fairly. The 2019 data revealed a significant gap in the time devoted to housework in dual-income households: husbands spent 54 minutes compared to their wives who spent 187 minutes. One study suggests that this disparity arises because women see embracing masculinity as a positive aspect, while men perceive embracing femininity not as an additional characteristic but as a threat to their masculinity. This mismatch becomes a complicating factor in marriage as it fails to fulfill the needs of both genders adequately.

Outlook & Implications

Two decades ago, a refrigerator commercial made waves with the memorable tagline, "The happiness of being a woman." This concise line hinted at the notion that the kitchen and refrigerator were predominantly a woman's domain. Fast forward more than 20 years, and LG Electronics' "Dios Objet Collection" advertisement exudes a distinctively transformed vibe. Advertisements like "Romantic Mood Maker," in which a husband prepares dinner for his wife, or "Fantastic Mood Maker," where he engages with his child, now showcase husbands and fathers who differ considerably from their predecessors. The core function of the refrigerator remains unchanged, but the people using it have evolved significantly over the past two decades.

Certainly, it's essential to approach the evolving role of husbands in contemporary society with caution. This means refraining from making sweeping generalizations about the blurring of gender boundaries and changes in daily life. In reality, gender disparities still exist, and it's important to acknowledge that these differences aren't necessarily wrong. Additionally, individuals may choose to adhere to traditional gender roles based on their values and circumstances, and it's crucial to respect their choices. It's also essential to recognize the increasing diversity in family structures. We should not overlook various family arrangements, including childless couples, singles, and children raised by grandparents, in our societal discussions. These evolving family dynamics deserve attention and consideration in our evolving social landscape.

However, there is widespread recognition of a pressing issue in Korean society: the declining birth rate. The solution to this issue is quite apparent: "We must foster a society conducive to raising children!" Many aspects of our daily lives still require significant changes. For instance, even when fathers patiently wait in line at the pediatrician's office, the child's medical forms distributed at hospitals often still request the mother to complete them. Additionally, male employees considering childcare leave often worry foremost about how their superiors will react. If we are to address these challenges effectively, we must not rely solely on the determination of men; we need to initiate cultural changes as well.

There are some more survey results worth considering. According to the results of a survey conducted by the Korean Peninsula Population Institute한반도미래인구연구원 for the Future, together with the research company Embrain, among unmarried 20- to 39-year-olds, 60.2% of those with high job satisfaction had an intention to have children, while 45.2% of those with low job satisfaction had a clear intention. At this time, factors that increased job satisfaction were "free use of annual leave" (70.8%), "guaranteed parental leave" (63.0%), and "fair treatment of employees returning after giving birth" (56.9%). Ultimately, a parenting-friendly corporate culture increases job satisfaction and makes people think positively about childrearing.

In May 2023, a news story about an SK On employee's wife giving birth to quadruplets, a first-time occurrence in Korea, generated significant attention. What's truly remarkable in this case isn't just the quadruplets themselves, but the fact that the decision to have children was influenced by the husband's employment at this company. The wife explained, "I heard that SK was a good company for starting and raising a family," and she actively pursued fertility treatments after her husband changed jobs. Notably, SK On supported this journey by allowing employees to accompany their wives to hospital visits weekly, thanks to flexible working hours and vacation time that employees could utilize without needing approval from superiors. They also provided substantial financial assistance for childbirth, greatly easing the burden of welcoming quadruplets. This case vividly illustrates how much support husbands can provide during childbirth and childrearing.

Furthermore, the market should proactively develop products and services catering to dads involved in childcare. In Japan, products like infant and toddler foods, designed for simplicity, have gained popularity since the implementation of a policy promoting men's participation in maternity leave, known as "postpartum paternity산후 파파육아," which began in 2022. These products include "liquid baby formula," which can be consumed conveniently without the hassle of preparing powdered formula, especially during late nights or outings, as well as porridge that can be quickly prepared by mixing ingredients and microwaving for just 1-2 minutes. In the United States, the company "Fathercraft" emerged because there was a lack of diaper bags designed for fathers; that is, ones that they could carry without feeling embarrassed. Beyond creating diaper bags that can function as backpacks and shoulder bags, they now offer reviews of baby products and online classes for expectant fathers.

The reader's reaction to this chapter is likely to vary depending on their age, gender, and whether they have sons or daughters. Younger readers may respond with, "It's not a new trend; it's already become normalized," while others might express concerns like, "But still, men are traditionally seen as the head of the household. Isn't this going a bit far?" Meanwhile, older individuals might adopt a more accepting perspective, saying, "Let them live as they please." These diverse reactions stem from personal experiences and positions in life.

However, what's truly essential is our commitment to offering personal and social support, regardless of whether we personally agree with these changes. This support is crucial to making it easier for young people to marry, have children, and lead happier lives. Each generation strives for happiness to the best of their ability, given their circumstances. Ultimately, isn't the very reason for a community's existence rooted in supporting the efforts of the younger generation?

Expanding Your Horizons:
Spin-off Projects

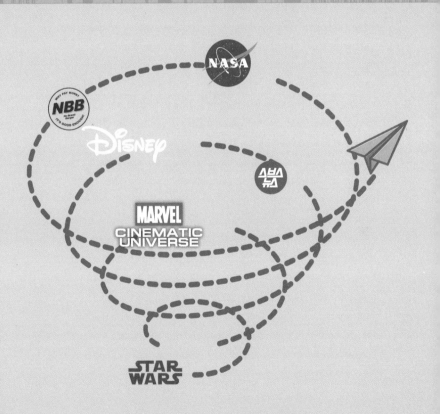

The dictionary definition of "spin off" is "to derive from" and "to separate (by centrifugal force)," as in spinning a thread from a cocoon. In the content industry, a "spin-off" is a "work that is derived from a specific source material," and is often used in movies and TV shows. We can see spin-offs from the Marvel Universe, such as the *Avengers* or *Spiderman* series, as important sources of creativity to build on that universe's worldview. The concept of spin-offs has recently expanded into the fields of branding, technology, organizational management, and personal career development, which we will refer to as "spin-off projects."

Brand spin-offs are popular when a company wants to reach new customers and markets while maintaining its existing brand identity. Premium fashion brands often launch sub-brands to cater to younger consumers or the "masstige" ("mass" + "prestige") market, while general brands can leverage their existing name recognition to enter new areas. Technology can also produce spin-offs. ARPAnet, which was developed by the U.S. Department of Defense as an alternative communications network, is a prime example of this. Companies are also eager to spin off new products. They foster new technologies, products, and business models through in-house ventures and spin them off if they are deemed successful. Individuals can also start spin-offs. Recently, side projects have become popular among employees, but they are not mere side hustles. A side project is an attempt to develop and apply self-development that can lead to a new career as an extension of one's current job.

As long as we continue to try to grow and respond to disruptive trends, spin-offs will become more and more popular as a way to create new businesses and for us to grow into more capable people.

"If you can dream it, you can do it. Always remember that this whole thing was started with a dream and a mouse."

– Walt Disney

By Walt Disney's own admission, his content kingdom started with a mouse. From the character Mickey Mouse, the company expanded to include cartoons, animation, movies, theme parks, and more. A 1957 memo from founder Walt Disney gives us a glimpse into how he envisioned growing the company and its brand by expanding and connecting its diverse content. Called the "synergy map" or the "Disney recipe," the memo exemplifies a cross-sightedness that pinpoints future market trends, provides insight into the company's unique and valuable assets, and considers connections to neighboring industries.

From Mickey Mouse and his girlfriend Minnie Mouse, to Pluto the dog, Donald Duck, and Goofy, Disney has evolved from a single mouse to a multitude of characters and content spin-offs. In the dictionary, "spin off" means "to derive from" or "to separate (by centrifugal force)," like thread from a cocoon, but in the realm of content creation, it refers to the extension of a work or character from an original source.

Now, the concept of spin-offs has expanded to include branding, technology, organizational management, and personal career development. In the age of multiplatforming, as distribution platforms multiply, products and brands, like content, are increasingly relying on spin-offs to create expansive worlds and engage passionate fans. In an era of explosive growth in technology in each field, especially in the space and military fields, the original technology is transformed and spun off to meet the needs of consumers. Above all, the rapidly changing market environment has made it more urgent for many organizations and individuals to quickly separate and derive more specialized capabilities based on their basic content or business. We will refer to this expanding concept of spin-offs in various fields as "spin-off projects."

Unlike pivoting, which is a complete change in business model, spin-offs can be labeled as "projects" because they are a series of activities that expand, combine, and flexibly change the business. If pivoting, as introduced in *Consumer Trend Insights 2021*, is a company-wide, front-to-back shift in business direction, spin-offs are fundamentally different in that they sow a variety of new possibilities, while keeping the core business area intact. In other words, spin-offs are a way to diversify and make your business more flexible by gradually shifting the center of gravity of the core business. In 2021, the business environment was shaken to its core by the prolonged COVID-19 pandemic, and some industries were forced to pivot. However, in an endemic era, where the pandemic has subsided and new business opportunities, including artificial intelligence, are emerging, spin-offs are a less risky and more stable strategy that allows for diversification while maintaining a business's core.

Content Spin-offs

As mentioned above, spin-offs originated in the entertainment sector, where they are still most active. In this context, a spin-off is a new story that takes place in the same universe as the original, encompassing the concepts of "prequel" and "sequel". Spin-offs can be broadly categorized as "prequels" that take place in the past, "sequels" that take place in the future, or even "reboots" that start with a new cast. The *Star Wars* movie franchise is a prime example of spin-offs, and since the first installment was released in 1977, it has continued to generate a strong worldwide fanbase. Fans of the original films naturally become fans of the spin-offs, and audiences who first encounter the spin-offs become interested in the original films and eventually become immersed in the world of the series. As a result, spin-offs deepen and broaden audience loyalty.

As content is increasingly available in a variety of mediums and forms, spin-offs have come to be characterized as trans-media, crossing various fields such as film, drama, comics, animation, and games. In particular, franchise spin-offs are all the rage in mainstream cinema today. This is a commercial strategy in which a large media franchise, such as Disney, develops and expands its original intellectual property (IP) into other media such as movies, dramas, novels, animations, and games. The *Star Trek, Transformers*, and *Star Wars* franchises all share one giant worldview, with spin-offs that continue the story as the universe expands.

The Marvel Cinematic Universe series began production in 2007, and as of September 2023, 32 films have been released, with 15 more planned for phases five and six. The 27 films released between 2008 and 2021 have grossed $23.5 billion at the global box office, making it the highest-grossing franchise of all time.

Why are spin-offs so prevalent in the content space? For starters, there's the advantage of being based on existing popular characters or content, which reduces box office risk. With the cost of content production rising astronomically, investors prefer to have a minimum amount of security to get their money back, and time-tested, existing content can provide that. Media consumption behavior has changed dramatically since the COVID-19 pandemic, with audiences preferring content that is guaranteed to be entertaining to some degree. With the expansion of OTT platforms such as Netflix and the increase in movie ticket prices, theaters are having a hard time attracting audiences. As a result, the movie industry is focusing on franchises that can retain fans with proven stories and characters.

As consumers enjoy the original content in different ways, they become fans of the work, which has the effect of perpetuating the life of the content. Ultimately, this network of original works and spin-offs forms a "worldview세계관," which can create a virtuous cycle that continually incorporates younger people as new consumers.

Branded Spin-offs

The concept of spin-offs basically refers to derivative works of content, but it's also being used to create products and brands. Through spin-offs, brands can broaden their target audience or flexibly change their brand image, increasing their scalability and preventing their image from becoming stale.

In particular, we often see luxury and premium fashion brands spin off secondary brands to target younger Generation MZ consumers or to launch "masstige" products, which are slightly cheaper premium products. Prada spun off its "Miu Miu" brand to create a younger, more sophisticated image. Maison Margiela spun off a brand called "MM6," which appeals to Generation MZ consumers with its quirky, streetwise image. Chloé also launched "See by Chloé," which is more casual than the original brand. British fashion brand DAKS launched "DAKS 10," positioning itself as a younger version of the classic and modern style of the existing DAKS brand and targeting millennial consumers. In the same vein, the fashion division of Samsung C&T spun off "KUHO Plus" from its women's brand KUHO, which also focuses on millennials. And LF launched its in-house venture brand "Dunst," a street-casual brand emphasizing youthful sensibilities.

Even if you're not a premium brand, spin-offs are a popular way for companies to diversify their business while effectively leveraging the recognition of their existing brand. Shinsegae Group's cost-effective food line, No Brand, spun off "No Brand Burger" in 2019 and received a good response from the market, exceeding 200 store openings within three and a half years of its launch, while SPC Group's bakery brand Paris Baguette spun off "Deli-cious델리셔스," a brand specializing in deli products such as sandwiches and salads. McDonald's announced plans to launch "CosMc's," a spin-off brand featuring smaller stores in the U.S., in 2024.

Spin-offs in the media industry are also active. With

the ever-growing reach of social media, YouTube creators and micro-influencers have become highly influential, and the influence of traditional media such as TV is relatively waning. As such, major broadcasters have been spinning off various media by boldly breaking away from traditional media formats and styles. MBC spun off "14F일사에프," which communicates with viewers through various channels such as YouTube, Facebook, Instagram, and TikTok. KBS's "KLAB크랩" and *JoongAng Ilbo*'s "Listen Smart Life (*deud-ddok-ra듣똑라*)" are both targeting the younger generations who are interested in trends and finance by presenting news in an easy and entertaining way on various channels. Each of their main YouTube channels has 480,000 and 400,000 subscribers, respectively.

The number of media spin-offs is increasing, as media outlets can attract new consumers by differentiating their content from the traditional format of channels. Furthermore, they can also expand their business opportunities by carving out new niches through a segmented approach to cater to different tastes of their audiences.

Successful spin-offs of a brand create a virtuous cycle where the brand's components become more diverse, attracting new fans of their brand, and ultimately building strong customer loyalty. However, when creating a new spin-off brand, it's important to make sure that it's distinct from the original brand and that it creates a positive feedback loop with the original brand. Many brands create spin-offs to expand their target audience, but they don't want to tarnish the image of the original brand in the process. For example, luxury fashion brand Chanel does not launch a menswear line. This is because the launch of a menswear line would compromise the unity and scarcity of the brand's image. Product and brand spin-offs should be carefully planned and executed to create a virtuous cycle in the long run.

Technology Spin-offs

"There's more space in your life than you think!" – *NASA*

Spin-offs are also an important concept in the technology development field. The National Aeronautics and Space Administration (NASA) refers to spin-offs as the application of its space technology to various industries. A typical example is the infrared ear thermometer, which is based on infrared temperature measurement technology originally developed by NASA to measure the temperature of stars. Freeze-dried food also comes from space food. Space food sublimates the moisture in food in a vacuum at ultra-low temperatures, allowing it to retain its shape and texture for longer periods of time, and has since been used in ramen soup, instant coffee, and dried fruit. In addition, memory foam was developed to improve the chairs and absorb shock for NASA's test pilots and is now used in various fields such as medicine and furniture, including bed mattresses, pillows, and cushions. NASA annually summarizes spin-offs related to project development and provides information on its website (spinoff.nasa.gov), which lists more than 2,000 examples of real-world products developed from NASA's original technologies since 1976.

In addition to space technology, military technology is often applied to industries. The current internet is an application of the military network ARPAnet, which was developed by the U.S. Department of Defense as an alternative communications network that could operate when partially damaged. In the immediate aftermath of World War II, passenger airplanes with jet fighter engine technology led to the explosive growth of the civilian aviation market, and the microwave oven was developed by Raytheon, a company specializing in radar, after a serendipitous discovery during research related to electromagnetic waves. Computers created for use in space development, weapons and ship control, and cryptography are other examples of defense technology transferred to civilian applications.

Similar types of technology spin-offs occur in commercial companies. Canon, a company that originally manufactured microscopes, evolved its business into office equipment such as copiers and printers by utilizing its core technology of optical precision. Such cases of technology spin-offs are expected to become more active and widespread in the future due to the development of advanced digital technologies such as artificial intelligence.

Organizational Spin-offs

As startups become a new economic engine, the creation of internal ventures is spreading across large companies. According to the Korea International Trade Association, the average age of a company was 61 years in 1958, but it is expected to drop to 12 years by 2027, a whopping five-fold decrease. Large companies are more vulnerable to crises because their organizations are large and decision making takes longer, and it is difficult to create a flexible organizational culture to discover new businesses in a rapidly changing business environment. To compensate for this rigidity, many large companies are systematically trying to establish internal ventures. In-house ventures can leverage the parent company's infrastructure and funding, giving them a leg up on other startups. Furthermore, by providing incentives for employees to commercialize their own ideas, they can improve their job satisfaction and inspire Generation MZ's desire for fairness.

Corporate spin-off startups are a type of corporate

venturing activity in which a new company is established externally based on internal corporate entrepreneurship to create economic value using new opportunities within the company.

In 2017, the "Pokémon Go" craze swept the world. You could see people on the streets with their phones, trying to catch virtual Pokémon. Niantic, the company behind "Pokémon Go," started as an internal Google venture. John Hanke, a Google VP, started Niantic in 2010 and spun it off in 2015. Since 2016, Niantic has been a huge success with "Pokémon Go," and in less than a year the company was valued at over $3.65 billion. In-house ventures are an efficient way to build a new business in a short period of time. eBay spun off PayPal, a company with a bright future, and grew it into a global company through independent operations. In 2016, Fiat Chrysler spun off Ferrari, making the Italian luxury sports car maker a standalone company to allow for greater autonomy and direction.

Korean conglomerates are also making great efforts to foster in-house ventures. Samsung Electronics has been discovering startups since 2012 through an in-house venture fostering program called "C-Lab Inside," and has implemented a spin-off system that allows in-house venture projects with the potential to excel to spin off into startups. Successful teams receive a minimum of 500 million won and a maximum of 1 billion won in business funding, and even if they leave the company after spinning off, they are given the opportunity to rejoin the company within five years. Since 2000, Hyundai Motor Group has operated an in-house startup incubation program called "Venture Plaza." In 2021, it changed its name to "ZERO1NE Company Builder제로원 컴퍼니 빌더" and expanded the scope of its business selection to various fields beyond automobiles. Selected startups receive up to 300 million won in development costs and have one year to develop and commercialize products and services before deciding whether to spin off or commercialize in house. There is also an opportunity to re-enter the program up to three years after the spin-off. A total of 76 teams have been selected through the program, and as of 2023, 30 companies have spun off independently. LG Electronics operates the in-house venture program "Studio 341." Domestic employees with creative ideas in various promising industries such as AI, smart homes, digital healthcare, robotics, and the metaverse are eligible, and the members of the five final selected teams are separated from their current jobs to focus on internal venture work in a separate off-site office where each team receives up to 400 million won in support.

Personal Career Spin-offs

Spin-offs are also happening on a personal level. More and

more people are looking to spin off their careers outside of their day jobs, and many are diving headfirst into side projects. While the term "side project" originally referred to developing new software in the tech space, it has expanded to include working on one's own projects informally and producing deliverables. A side project is different from a simple side hustle. If you deliver food or drive a car after work for extra cash, that's not a side project. A side project is when you set aside personal time to pursue something related to what you do at work or a separate area of interest. People can use side projects as an opportunity to create new careers, practice self-improvement that they may not have been able to do at work, and, if successful, lead to entrepreneurship or a career change.

A side project is also different from a hobby or leisure activity. It's literally a project, an intentional activity with specific goals, an organized plan, and the resolve to reach those goals step by step. It's not something you do in your spare time, it's more of a labor that you intentionally put time and effort into. It's all about experimenting with what you want to do to realize your value. As such, side projects are more about personal growth.

Many of the spin-offs mentioned above also started as side projects. Naver, a leading platform company, started as an internal venture of Samsung SDS; Twitter started as an internal hackathon; and Daangn was a side project of Kakao developers. Many people who have successfully launched side projects emphasize the importance of maintaining a full-time job. In the same way that the concept of a spin-off is to do something that doesn't harm the original work, side projects also emphasize parallelism with the main business. You don't want to abandon your day job too soon when you start a side project, but rather work alongside it for a while. It's important to spin off the experience and skills you've gained in your day job to run a side project, and to continually explore the possibilities for success.

It's becoming increasingly common for companies to encourage side projects rather than dismiss them as a "distraction (slacking딴짓)." Microsoft officially encourages side projects. Microsoft has dozens of side projects running in parallel through its garage program. Side projects can be completely unrelated to your main job. This allows employees to help themselves grow and recognize that their work contributes directly or indirectly to the development of the Microsoft Corporation.

Is it acceptable in Korean organizational culture for an individual to work on a side project to spin off his or her career? The trend of career spin-offs is likely to become a major issue in organizational and human resource management in the future. Most organizations expect their employees to stick to their main job, and many of them stipulate "no second job겸업금지" and "no for-profit activities" through employment rules. However, the "capitalist kids" are now looking for their pipeline (income stream) not only from their paychecks, but also from the momentum of their own growth to move on and start their own businesses. How do you manage side projects to create synergies that benefit both the company and its people? Organizations and individuals alike are facing some very difficult questions.

Outlook and Implications

Rebranding for spin-offs

It's not uncommon for companies to change their name these days. Maeil Dairy매일유업 is considering dropping "Dairy" from its name. This is because the company is trying to change its core business from the past dairy-centered business structure in the era of a declining birthrate and aging population, and is focusing on alternative milk and protein supplements, as well as food service businesses such as coffee shop "Paul Bassett" and authentic Cantonese restaurant "Crystal Jade." The company is trying to diversify its business direction by facing the reality of the specification industry and predicting what the promising industries will be in the future. Kia Motors also changed its name to "KIA" in 2021 to expand its business beyond electric vehicles to become a mobility company with innovative technologies. Market Kurly마켓 컬리 changed its name to "Kurly컬리" and began operating under two categories of services: "Market Kurly" and "Beauty Kurly." As the company has been strengthening its capabilities in fresh food, it has also revealed its strategy to expand its business into non-food categories such as beauty and household products. Samyang Food Group's삼양식품 name change to "Samyang Roundsquare삼양라운드스퀘어" and Lotte Confectionery's name change to "Lotte Wellfood롯데웰푸드" can be understood in a similar context. In short, simplifying the name can be interpreted as an intention to reflect the parent brand in the event of frequent spin-offs in the future.

This trend is a global phenomenon. Dunkin' boldly dropped "Donuts" from its brand name to avoid being perceived as a place that only sells donuts. Similarly, Starbucks removed "STARBUCKS COFFEE" from its logo. The trend is toward simpler brand logos to encompass a wider range of future business areas. It's becoming increasingly important for brands to have a flexible identity that can spin off into different industries and areas. Facebook, which changed its name to "Meta," and Intel, which is expanding its business beyond PCs to IoT, are also accelerating their rebranding efforts to encompass new future businesses.

If independence or spin-off from a parent company is understanding spin-offs in the narrow sense, then rebranding, which involves re-conceptualizing and repositioning a brand, can be seen as a spin-off in the broader sense, or as "keeping the door open" for a spin-off down the line. Re-branding is now becoming an essential preliminary task for spin-offs that respond to changing trends over time. Spin-offs are a strategy to enhance brand diversity and flexibility and expand business models in a changing market environment. Through spin-offs, companies seek to diversify risk and avoid failure through continuous change.

The problem with overusing spin-offs

Of course, spin-offs are not a panacea. Whether it's a movie or a brand, a mechanical spin-off that lacks freshness and creativity will not resonate with the public and consumers. If a spin-off tries to force itself to resonate with the public while ignoring their tastes, it will be disliked and fail. By anticipating future market changes and creatively combining disparate elements and exploring new territories, it is important to think deeply about how to evoke public empathy and market response.

When companies, especially platform companies, spin off, they need to pay close attention to issues such as monopolization and encroachment on side markets. Especially for large platform companies such as Kakao and Naver, which have a dominant position in the market, spin-offs are a very effective way to diversify and expand their business. However, excessive and reckless expansion requires careful consideration, as they may face strong criticism for encroaching on local businesses or for monopoly issues. The case of Naver illustrates the importance of socially responsible management for large IT companies. In 2012, Naver launched an open marketplace service called ShopN, which was criticized for infringing on the rights of online mom-and-pop shops온라인 골목상권. Within two years of its launch, Naver withdrew ShopN and introduced Store Farm (now Smart Store), a service with zero entry fees. The elimination of sales commissions and the influx of entrepreneurs have revitalized Naver's shopping business, which has further strengthened the Naver ecosystem, including Naver Pay and Naver Plus membership. As such, platform giants should put more emphasis on coexistence with small and medium-sized enterprises (SMEs) as their social influence has increased.

If you're launching a spin-off, you'll need to know what your unique selling point (USP) is and apply it. Whether it's a corporate rebrand or a personal side project, a spin-off is a brand extension. When extending a brand, it's important to consider the core quality and relevance of the original product so that it can be synergized with subsequent product or line extensions. The same lessons can apply for individuals. Just like a successful brand extension strategy, a personal spin-off requires a strategic approach to planning and executing the spin-off to check the current capabilities and positioning of the personal brand and create a virtuous feedback loop with the main business.

Rita Gunther McGrath, a professor at Columbia University, advocates for a "transient advantage" strategy, where the pace of change and connectivity accelerates and necessitates constant experimentation to find answers quickly. A more complex and flexible strategic posture is critical. She emphasized the importance of change and connectivity in the battle arena, and that spin-off strategies that enhance diversity and flexibility through expansion and combination will be more effective tactics in this arena.

Spin-offs are a form of tuning, a process of expanding and changing your offerings and fine-tuning yourself in the face of ever-changing public tastes and market conditions. New products and new business opportunities always arise in the tiny cracks of the mainstream market. Spin-offs are the best way to capitalize on these niche opportunities and respond quickly. Spin-offs are dynamic. Organizations and individuals who diligently sow multiple seeds, explore possibilities, and look at future opportunities from multiple angles will eventually be the ones to take advantage of them. Spin-offs will continue to be a key strategy for sustaining growth in the face of prolonged low growth and constant change for many years to come.

You Choose, I'll Follow:
Ditto Consumption

In the age of excess, with a surge in products and purchase options, consumers face abundant choices. In response, they adopt a new way of consuming, bypassing traditional decision-making processes and instead follow choices proposed by a specific proxy – an individual, content type, or commerce channel, which is known as "ditto consumption." This differs from blindly following a star or influencer; it's a more subjective following based on an alignment with one's personal values.

The first thing ditto consumers follow are individuals. Not only do they agree with the purchases of influencers they follow on social media, but they also click the purchase button without hesitation for products recommended by experts or employees of manufacturing and sales companies. The second thing they follow is specific content. They buy clothes and accessories based on the style of their favorite webtoon's male and female protagonists, and they decide to travel to places featured in certain dramas or movies. The last thing they follow is a commerce channel, the path to purchase. They buy based on suggestions from "vertical" shops that sell specific product lines with unique, discerning tastes.

The rise of ditto consumption is tied to changes in the modern retail landscape. Product variety and distribution channels have expanded, quality has leveled off, and the abundance of choice and the fear of better option (FOBO) have surged. With brand loyalty waning, following favorite individuals, content, and commerce channels has become a more satisfying heuristic than following a manufacturer or brand. The proliferation of ditto consumption affects distribution strategies and business model development. Rather than solely competing based on product quality, a "signature" product or brand embodying a company's philosophy, perspective, and taste serves as a flagship to navigate the waves of ditto consumption.

"I've always loved you." — "Ditto."

When the male protagonist, Sam (played by Patrick Swayze), says, "I've always loved you," the female protagonist, Molly (played by Demi Moore), replies, "Ditto." This is a line from the 1990 movie *Ghost*, which was so popular that it even spawned a musical. The line "oh, say it ditto" also appears in the song 'Ditto' by the popular girl group New Jeans뉴진스 – they're essentially asking their listeners: "Tell me you like me too."

The use of "ditto" is increasing not only in confessions of love, but also in the process of purchasing goods and services. In fact, purchasing is a sophisticated process that requires very complex decisions. First, the "recognition of the problem" of what to purchase is followed by the "information search," which involves all the cognitive functions of exposure, attention, perception, memory, learning, and attitude formation. Until a purchase is made, a rigorous "alternative evaluation" is conducted on the selected candidates. However, these days, the consumption phenomenon of skipping all these complicated procedures and simply following a specific person, type of content, or commerce channel and purchasing it with the thought, "Me too — ditto," is on the rise. In *Consumer Trend Insights 2024*, we would like to call this type of consumption "ditto consumption."

There are surprisingly many ways consumers buy clothes these days. People show their own consumption behavior in the face of more diverse options than ever before, such as those who buy from vintage shops, those who buy directly from overseas, those who buy from influencer brands they follow, and those who buy from resale platforms. We looked at how many shopping-related apps were installed on the smartphones of participants in a consumer focus group held at the Consumer Trend Center (CTC), and found there were between 30 to 50 apps installed. In this complex consumption environment, consumers choose a consumption method of following specific individuals, types of content, and commerce channels to make "ditto" purchases in order to minimize the effort of purchasing decisions.

Three Aspects of Ditto Consumption

1. Individual ditto

The first target that ditto consumers follow are individuals. In the past, it was important to ask, "Which brand and product do you own?", but these days, "Who uses the product?" is the more important question. This is because rather than the symbolism of the product or the brand itself, how the product is interpreted within the reference group, that is, the people who influence the ditto consumer, is now more important.

These days, the question of "Who is selling the product?" is becoming more important in second-hand transactions. Second-hand trading is evolving from simply buying necessary items at a low price to buying a seller's particular taste and style. Once you decide that a seller exhibits your taste in the second-hand trading app, you can then continue to purchase the collection of used goods he or she sells. Taking advantage of this trend, 'Depop', a second-hand trading platform that started in Italy and established itself in the UK, added a social-media-style interface to its sales function by providing Instagrammable photos of sellers. One-third of all consumers aged 15 to 24 in the UK are now registered with Depop.

The individual seller followed by ditto consumers assumes the role of a curator while imbuing their products with personal significance through their unique interpretations. This distinction sets "individual ditto consumption" apart from conventional fandom consumption and celebrity marketing. In the context of fandom consumption or celebrity endorsements, consumers often make purchases based on their admiration for a particular celebrity, unquestioningly opting for products endorsed or used by that celebrity. In contrast, within the realm of individual ditto consumption, a critical question emerges: "To what extent does this individual's lifestyle align with my own values?" In this scenario, the follower's subjective interpretations play a pivotal role in shaping the purchasing decision.

"Money can buy fashion, but it can't buy style"

The introductory text of 'Sister Choi Next Door옆집언니 최실장,' a YouTube channel specializing in fashion, styling, and shopping, emphasizes that how one uses a product is more important than the product itself. She introduces viewers to topics on how to properly coordinate and match fashion products and the essential items needed to accomplish this. She also shows viewers how to coordinate, combine, and store purchased products, giving precious tips on wearing denim, suits, and making fantastic combinations of T-shirts and necklaces. When it comes to essential items categorized by type, her straightforward and decisive approach, like "purchase vs. abstain 산다 vs. 안산다," can effectively address the issue. There are many styling influencers, but ditto consumers who follow 'Sister Choi Next Door' can expunge the overflowing options in their minds and make a purchase decision without hesitation because they have a firm and trusted proxy decision from Sister Choi on whether or not to purchase something.

Another type of individual to follow for ditto consumption is an expert with a lot of knowledge in a specific field. In addition to the fashion field, content that recommends products based on expertise across all fields, including pharmacists, medical specialists, makeup artists, and IT experts, is gaining popularity. Consumers can now meet experts more easily than ever through various social media and video platforms, and can directly ask experts about things they are curious about in their daily lives. Experts aid in decision-making by pinpointing consumer needs through their extensive industry knowledge. Rather than relying on uncertain information gathered through online searches, ditto consumers gravitate towards active online experts, including renowned doctors, makeup artists, and stylists, who provide valuable guidance.

As people-centered content gains popularity, many companies are shifting their marketing strategies towards utilizing their own employees. For example, Lush Korea, a handmade cosmetics retailer, operates a YouTube channel where employees from various branches respond to customer inquiries about products and recommend suitable items for different situations. Convenience store chain CU posts videos of its employees reviewing new products every week, and cosmetics select shop Olive Young operates "AllYoung

TV올영TV," which features a medical doctor with eight years of experience. Hyundai Card Newsroom uploads friendly YouTube videos that show what credit cards Hyundai Card employees use. In response to this trend, the novel term, "employencer" (a blend of "employee" and "influencer"), has emerged. These employencers wield significant influence on social media platforms, garnering substantial engagement from ditto consumers owing to their in-depth knowledge of the company's products and their relatable, human approach. In fact, 53% of survey respondents from around the world said that they get reliable information about a company directly from company employees. This approach differs from conventional advertising, as it doesn't involve official company-level promotions. Instead, it humanizes individual employees within the company, aiming to elicit a response from consumers on a more personal level.

Individuals who share similar tastes are another type of individual ditto consumption. Ditto consumers follow Instagram accounts that align with their preferences and make purchasing decisions by browsing through their posts. Social media, which was originally intended for social interaction, now serves as a personalized, curated magazine of content that resonates with one's unique tastes. In contrast to commercial magazines that are curated by editors in a one-size-fits-all way, ditto consumers' Instagram accounts can be seen as personalized magazines or scrapbooks, directly tailored to individual preferences. From ordinary people to celebrities, anyone with similar tastes can become a target of ditto consumption.

Celebrities' fashion styles have always been of interest to the public. Now, separate from their official social media accounts, Instagram accounts that collect only fashion or makeup style information of specific celebrities of interest have been created, making it easier for ditto consumers to make choices. Examples include the 'jendeukiestyles' Instagram account, which collects the stylings of Blackpink's Jennie, and the 'joysstyles' Instagram account, where you can follow the fashion choices of Red Velvet's Joy. But these are all accounts created by fans, not by the artist or their agents. These styling accounts provide the brand, product name, and pricings of all items worn by the celebrity, showcasing fashion styles worn in concert, or spotted at the airport, as well as daily fashion selfies posted on artists' personal social media.

The concept of "individual ditto consumption" extends beyond celebrities and influencers; it encompasses ordinary people in our daily lives who can be invaluable in shaping purchase decisions. For instance, travel enthusiasts generously share their mapped-out routes, neatly organizing everything from itineraries to recommended restaurants. This empowers ditto consumers to embark on their own journeys with confidence, benefiting from these practical insights.

In the quest for exceptional dining experiences, someone's "My Own Good Restaurant Map^{나만의 맛집 지도}" will be helpful in pinpointing outstanding restaurants on platforms like Naver Maps or Kakao Maps. Consumers who fail to find exceptional dining spots solely through traditional searches and ratings actively use such curated maps as reliable sources of information.

The number of followers required to become an "individual ditto" influencer followed by ordinary consumers can vary, but there is a prevailing consensus among various consulting and research companies that being a "nano-influencer" with less than 10,000 followers is typically sufficient. This is primarily because the influence of motivating followers to engage in ditto consumption is often more significant than having a large follower count. Nano-influencers possess a unique identity compared to influencers with larger followings, enabling them to deliver more pertinent content to their followers and build closer, more personal relationships with them. These distinctive characteristics enable nano-influencers to elicit a richer response from followers who share similar tastes.

In the context of ditto consumption, the key drivers are the alignment of tastes and the bond with followers, rather than sheer fame. Consequently, when aiming to raise awareness, macro or mega-influencers with substantial followers may be more suitable. However, if the goal is to drive purchases through ditto consumption, focusing on nano-influencers or micro-influencers is often more effective, as they can establish a more intimate connection with their audience.

2. Content ditto

The second category of what people follow is content. From simple concerns such as what to have for dinner to somewhat complex concerns such as where to go on vacation, people are increasingly seeking answers in various forms of media such as comics, dramas, and movies. This phenomenon has become more noticeable since the COVID-19 period, when content consumption had surged due to increased time spent at home. This immersion in content also affects the real world beyond our screens. While the original intent of consumable content was simply for entertainment and enjoyment, content has begun to evolve into a factor that tangibly impacts ditto consumers' consumption choices.

One of the biggest draws for watching HBO's *Euphoria*, which has captured the hearts of Generation MZ around the world, is the characters' stylings. Since its first airing in 2019, the "*Euphoria* look" has solidified itself as a fashion genre unto itself and has been playing its role as a style reference for Gen MZ for several years. According to a CNN article published in April 2023, there were thousands of videos tagged with #euphoriaoutfits on TikTok alone, and they were played over 28 million times on various social media platforms. Users share their own fashion that imitates *Euphoria*'s styles, and also share purchase information on items worn by the drama's main characters.

The area where content-driven ditto consumption is most conspicuous is travel. According to a 2023 survey conducted by global reservation platform Expedia, movies and dramas were identified as the most influential media on travel destination choices, surpassing the impact of social media. A striking 66% of consumers worldwide considered set locations featured in movies and dramas as travel destinations, with 39% of them subsequently making reservations. Additionally, according to the airline ticket service Kayak, the number of British people searching for airline tickets to Korea increased by 50% after Netflix's *Squid Game*오징어게임 aired. Notably, the keyword that witnessed an overwhelming surge in search volume on Google Trends was "Jeju Island," a destination mentioned by the North Korean defector in the show as a place she aspired to visit someday.

So-called "set-jetting," which involves following and visiting locations featured in movies or dramas, is a typical example of content-inspired ditto consumption. As set-jetting has emerged as a hot topic in the travel industry, packages and tour products that combine content and tourism are being released one after another. Actually, set-jetting is not a wholly new phenomenon. However, what differentiates content-driven ditto consumption from past "set location pilgrimages" is that it goes beyond a two-dimensional trip to visit the set locations of movies or dramas and provides a three-dimensional experience of immersing oneself in the universe or worldview세계관 of a particular piece of content.

Importantly, content-driven ditto consumers take an active role in interpreting the content's worldview. A recent case in point is the release of the film *Asteroid City* by renowned director Wes Anderson, celebrated for his mastery of colors and composition. Fans who watched the movie appeared to absorb the director's distinctive fairytale-like color palette and inject it into their social media posts. While in the past, people simply admired the director's use of colors, now they edit their own photos and videos with similar colors by using shared color correction methods and camera app filters. Some ditto consumers go further and upload Instagram reels containing Anderson's unique style, encompassing fonts, background music, and symmetrical video compositions, among other elements.

Content-driven ditto consumption is not confined to content that exclusively features real people. The recent advancement of animation, webtoons, and web novels is reshaping the landscape of content-driven ditto consumption trends, which were once primarily enjoyed by a niche group of enthusiasts. For example, the works of Studio Ghibli, famous for their mouth-watering depictions of food, are one answer to today's consumers' question, "What should I eat?" For example, if you search for *"Howl's Moving Castle* food" on social media or YouTube, you'll find recipes for dishes featured in the animation, or information about restaurants that serve such menu items. This phenomenon goes beyond merely following. In the past, for example, visiting restaurants in cooking-themed cartoons was the method of content-driven ditto consumption. However, now people want to copy the food in the animation involving no cooking at all, reproducing it perfectly on their table. This represents a facet of ditto consumption where consumers seek to immerse themselves within the unique worldviews presented in the animations.

In recent times, popular webtoons have become a significant focus of ditto consumption. What's intriguing is the growing trend of emulating not just the fashion but also the makeup styles of cartoon characters. In fact, there's a YouTube channel that has garnered popularity by instructing viewers on how to replicate the makeup looks of female webtoon protagonists. With the rising prevalence of ditto consumption related to webtoons, some brands have even begun to offer product placement opportunities within these popular webtoons, recognizing the potential for impactful marketing through this medium.

3. Commerce channel ditto

The final type of ditto consumption is following a distribution or commerce channel. Even in the domain of online and mobile shopping, consumers are demonstrating an increasing preference for specialized stores that exclusively focus on specific product categories, rather than opting for large, all-encompassing retailers. These specialized outlets are commonly referred to as "vertical commerce" establishments, owing to their vertical specialization: they meticulously curate and showcase products with a distinct and refined taste, specifically tailored to the preferences of their target audience. While there are slight differences among "editorial shops편집숍," "select stores셀렉트숍," "taste shops취향숍," and "curation shops큐레이션숍" in Korea, they each adhere to particular standards and contexts that define their individuality. This evolving consumer behavior can aptly be termed "commerce channel ditto consumption" as it entails following and purchasing products recommended by these vertical commerce entities.

"Point of View," a stationery boutique situated in the hip Seongsu neighborhood of Seoul, achieves an avant-garde ambiance with brief but thought-provoking quotes adorning the walls. Questions like "If you had to choose just one tool for your work, what would it be?" and "Which process do you start with first?" in the store are accompanied by sentences from famous writers such as Toni Morrison and

William Styron relating to the question. This has the uncanny ability of transforming shoppers into writers, at least for the duration of their in-store visit.

Within the store's confines, you find yourself in the company of ardent wordsmiths. It's intriguing how they manage to imbue the act of purchasing seemingly mundane items like erasers and pencils with a sense that one is acquiring the primal tools of storytelling. By embracing the creator's perspective presented at Point of View, the discerning consumer transcends the transactional aspect, instead investing in the interpretation and sensibilities intertwined with the stationery. Consequently, what would otherwise be ordinary stationery, available at any typical stationery store, assumes a special significance under the distinctive Point of View aura. Consumers align themselves with the stationery shop's prensentation, partaking in ditto consumption by following its curated point of view.

Much like Point of View encourages consumers to embrace their creative side, the travel accommodation booking platform Stayfolio empowers travelers to become "rest쉼표 explorers." Recognized as the epitome of unique and unforgettable stays, 'Stayfolio' curates experiences that set it apart from other platforms. Consider this vivid description of one of their properties: "Immerse yourself in warm waters while gazing upon a garden that evokes bygone emotions. Watch the yard transform as raindrops fall and snow blankets the landscape, allowing your mind to wander freely. Here, you can relish a leisurely, unhurried escape from the daily grind." This narrative paints a vivid and emotion-laden picture of the property, in stark contrast to the conventional, data-driven listings that merely list features like "2 bedrooms, 1 bathroom, free WiFi."

Stayfolio's unique interpretation of spaces also shines through in their photographs. With its emphasis on a tranquil ambiance and relaxation, the platform perfectly aligns with the preferences of modern consumers who consider accommodation not just as a necessity of travel but as a destination in itself.

Even when commerce channels don't explicitly convey individual tastes and preferences, they can still create an environment conducive to ditto consumption by cultivating a sense of community among its users. Take, for instance, Musinsa, an online fashion store, which operates "Musinsa Snap" – a unique feature where users can explore a diverse range of styles. Musinsa Snap, functioning as an "app within an app," grants user access to fashion curated from every day, well-dressed individuals, meticulously selected by Musinsa. This encompasses fashion enthusiasts found on the streets, staff members, and models associated with participating brands.

What's particularly intriguing here is that it transcends the mere appreciation of someone's clothing style. Instead, it delves into the narrative behind each fashion choice. In essence, it's not just about saying, "I admire their style, and I particularly like this aspect of their outfit," but rather, it's about saying, "I purchased this hat after a heated argument with my boyfriend during my trip to Japan..." – connecting with the personal stories woven into the garments. These consumer narratives infuse a commerce channel with an emotional depth, collectively shaping the overall "feel" of the shopping experience.

Background of Ditto Consumption

Complex consumption environment and anxious consumers

When people make purchasing decisions, what's the most appropriate number of options to choose from? In an experiment in 2000, Sheena Iyengar, a business professor (with a PhD in social psychology) at Columbia Business School, displayed six types of jam at one stand and 24 types of jam at another stand and observed customers' reactions. As a result of the experiment, the sales rate of the stand displaying six types of jam was approximately ten times higher than that of the stand displaying 24 types of jam. For consumers, having more options than necessary acts as a hindrance to their choice. However, the number of choices modern consumers face when making an actual purchase is not just a few dozen, but a few thousand. Let's take sneakers as an example. When searching for sneakers in the Naver portal search bar, consumers are instantly faced with more than 1,800 products. Not only product types but also distribution channels through which search terms are entered have become more diverse. In a society where time is more precious than ever, and efficiency is a highly prized commodity, it is paradoxical that the consumption environment has grown increasingly complex. As a result, consumers are confronted with a situation of choice overload and paralysis, making it all the more challenging for them to navigate their purchasing decisions.

The factors influencing product purchases have evolved significantly. In the past, product quality and price were the primary determinants of consumer choices. However, now consumers take into account a product's broader context, including the emotional or symbolic value it holds - dimensions that can be challenging to discern through conventional online searches. Even if a product offers exceptional quality and an appealing price point, it may be excluded from a consumer's consideration if it does not align with their sensibilities, personal preferences, or ethical values, such as those related to animal welfare or political correctness. In such cases, the product is promptly removed from the individual's shopping list.

The burden on consumers facing a complex consumption environment manifests itself as the FOBO (fear of better options) phenomenon. Consumers postpone a purchase decision because they are concerned that there may be a better option that they may have missed. In order to make the best decision, they must search for a vast amount of information and evaluate alternatives; but in situations where this process is not easy in practice, consumers sometimes opt to choose nothing rather than make a wrong choice. In particular, in a social atmosphere where efficiency is emphasized, the perceived greater opportunity cost of failure also leads to the FOBO phenomenon. Consumers who feel anxious in the complex consumer environment have come to search for new purchasing decision methods to make the optimal choice, even if they cannot make the best choice. As a result, consumers choose ditto consumption as an alternative, which involves finding and following an agent who will make the purchasing decisions on their behalf.

Wavering brand loyalty

The distribution market is undergoing a noticeable shift in power, marked by the disruption of traditional marketing conventions and norms. The emergence of social media such as Instagram has made connection and communication between consumers possible. As a result, consumers have come to be much more influenced by communication with people they meet through horizontal relationships online than by the vertical marketing communication that existing brands delivered across many sectors. Brands are also trying to break down existing walls and communicate with people on an equal footing.

The emergence of ditto consumption is intimately tied to this shifting power dynamic in the market. Unlike consumers of the past who had limited options and had to rely solely on brand narratives in an exclusive marketplace, today's consumers have access to a multitude of choices from diverse sources. Moreover, as quality standards have risen across the board, the notion of exclusively adhering to branded products has lost its significance.

According to a survey conducted by McKinsey, consumers are displaying an unprecedented rate of brand switching. The data reveals a substantial increase in the number of U.S. consumers who have experimented with new brands, soaring from 33% in September 2020 to a remarkable 46% by February 2022. This trend is not limited to brand loyalty alone; it extends to distribution channels as well. The percentage of consumers who have considered switching to different distribution channels climbed from 28% in September 2020 to 37% in February 2022.

This surge in brand and distribution channel exploration underscores the shifting landscape of consumer preferences. In this evolving environment, consumers increasingly prioritize personal factors, such as their specific situation and tastes, over brand loyalty when making purchasing decisions. Consequently, the concept of ditto consumption is garnering more attention, as it offers a means to navigate these changing dynamics and align consumer choices with individual preferences and circumstances.

Outlook and Implications

The light and shade of ditto consumption

Lately, with luxury brands like Chanel or Dior appointing brand ambassadors who are younger than ever before, there has been a surge in middle and high school students seeking luxury goods as gifts from their parents. The associated costs are often exorbitant, placing a significant financial burden on parents.

Appropriate ditto consumption offers the advantage of simplifying the complex decision-making process for consumers. However, inappropriate ditto consumption carries the risk of encouraging irrational spending habits among consumers. The scenario in which students seek luxury items without considering what they actually value in life themselves or what their family's economic circumstances are, is a prime example of such irrational consumption. Importantly, this issue is not confined to teenagers alone. The culture of flaunting one's possessions on social media platforms can drive even adult consumers to make purchases that exceed their genuine means and needs. Therefore, it's crucial to exercise caution, especially when the target of ditto consumption is a person or an influencer. Consumers must cultivate the ability to make independent consumption choices, grounded in objective judgment about the individuals they follow and their own financial situation.

Industrial response to ditto consumption

In the past, consumers compared as many products as possible in supermarkets and department stores, or in comprehensive online shopping malls, and then selected the product with the best value and quality. However, today, as the number of products and distribution channels has increased, and product quality has reached the same plateau, it has become difficult to induce ditto consumption simply because a product has excellent quality.

First, selection and concentration of marketing and sales are important. The first starting point would be to accurately set the target users for a product and develop micro-influencers and vertical commerce sites that fit that target, but as a prerequisite, a company or brand's own philosophy that goes beyond excellent product quality is now needed. This is because what ditto consumers truly want to follow is not simply the product but the perspective of the person they are following. The basis for consumers' ditto consumption is that they agree with the interpretation of the products proposed by the individuals, types of content, and commerce channels that are the targets of ditto consumption. In this situation, brands need to think about their own differentiated perspectives that will draw the attention of ditto consumers.

In light of these concerns, the significance of "signature products" has grown considerably. In the context of commerce, expressions like "signature __" are often used to refer to a product that a company or brand takes pride in presenting as a unique representation of their identity. In the era of increasingly active ditto consumption, where consumers are drawn to products and perspectives that align with their values, having a signature product becomes essential. While companies continue to introduce products that cater to various consumer needs, having a signature product that authentically expresses the company's identity is crucial.

For some companies, a signature product is viewed as a form of advertisement, one that eloquently conveys the company's perspective to consumers, even if it means sacrificing immediate sales profits. A notable example is LG Electronics, which has established "Signature" as a distinct brand. During the development of this brand, top management emphasized that it should be seen as an advertisement rather than a product for immediate sale, underlining the brand's primary purpose of conveying the company's identity and values to consumers. This underscores the evolving role of signature products as powerful tools for branding and communication in the age of ditto consumption.

In today's distribution market, where the influence of brands on purchasing decisions has waned compared to the past, the effective use of signature products serves as a means to offer consumers a fresh perspective on companies. Signature products play a significant role in alleviating customer decision fatigue. By presenting a singular signature option to consumers facing the daunting prospect of choice overload or FOBO, companies can assist them in making decisions with confidence.

In the planning of products and services, it's equally crucial to create an environment that facilitates the ease of following and purchasing. This entails establishing physical and psychological spaces where micro-influencers and ditto consumers can engage in active communication. As previously mentioned, ditto consumption hinges not solely on the product itself but on how customers interpret the philosophy of the company and brand. Consequently, it is incumbent upon companies to reevaluate their core principles and readdress that most fundamental question again: "What is the philosophy of our company and brand?"

ElastiCity:
Liquidpolitan

In an era of declining population, cities are at a tipping point. Regional trends are shifting from "fixed cities" where people settle down to "flexible cities" where diverse populations come together. New changes are unfolding in front of us, where local content flows, people move according to their lifestyles, and various possibilities manifest as they interact with each other. A city that flexibly transforms itself to attract people with its unique cultural capital and overflows with the synergy of diverse people will be called a "liquidpolitan" city.

Liquidpolitanism is not about building on a large scale. It is a series of projects that connect creatives. Particularly important are the roles of "signature stores" that represent an area by attracting people with their unique charm, "local entrepreneurs" who reimagine and transform the city, and "local creators" who transform the space by analyzing the commercial area and customers.

Now that we have passed the population "death cross," where the number of deaths is greater than the number of births, tactical urbanism that grows slowly through small experiments is more important than large-scale development based on the premise of population growth. The development of transportation that maximizes mobility between regions, and the emergence of the "floating generation" that pursues a fluid life, mark the importance of regional development based on the concept of liquid urbanism. Creating a livable city is not just about reviving depopulated areas, but also about creating a city with an open growth plate in terms of diversity and creativity. We look forward to the emergence of small but mighty liquidpolitan cities, each with their own unique charms, which are constantly experimenting with the possibilities of embracing diversity.

Mr. A, who has resided in his childhood home in Doksan-dong, Seoul, works as a developer at an IT company located in Pangyo, Gyeonggi-do. Over time, due to his activities primarily revolving around eating, watching movies, and socializing in Pangyo, he has essentially turned his Doksan-dong residence into a boarding house. Mr. A is also an avid surfer, and every weekend he embarks on surfing expeditions from his home to Yangyang, Gangwon-do. Recently, he relocated to a solo officetel in Misa-dong, Hanam City, to expedite his journey to Yangyang. This decision was prompted by his company granting him the opportunity to work at the Yangyang Workcation Center. For the past two months, Mr. A has been residing in Yangyang, dedicating his days to work and his mornings and evenings to the joys of surfing. His impending return to Pangyo next month has led him to contemplate whether to return to his parents' house in Doksan-dong or stay in an officetel in Misa-dong.

Is Mr. A a resident of Seoul, Gyeonggi-do, or Gangwon-do? According to government records, Mr. A's official residence is in Seoul, as he has been registered in Doksan-dong for an extended period. Economically speaking, he can be associated with Gyeonggi-do since his salary is paid in Pangyo, and most of his expenditures occur in that vicinity. Nevertheless, for the past two months and upcoming weekends, he has effectively been a resident of Gangwon-do due to his extensive time spent on workcation in Yangyang. So, let's ask again: Is Mr. A a resident of Seoul, Gyeonggi-do, or Gangwon-do?

As transportation becomes increasingly convenient and people's lifestyles become more flexible, the conventional concepts of residence and population are undergoing significant changes. Let's use Yangyang, the destination of Mr. A's weekend surfing trips, as an example. In Yangyang, a striking demographic contrast emerges: the population aged over 60 constitutes a substantial 45%, whereas those in their 20s and 30s account for a mere 14%. The total population stands at 27,822, with a relatively low birth rate of 0.88. From the perspective of a "settled population^{정주인구}," Yangyang-gun is categorized as a declining population area, facing the imminent threat of so-called "regional extinction."

However, when viewed through the lens of visitor influx, a surprising reversal occurs. In recent times, young individuals who relish surfing and revelry have been flocking to Yangyang, resulting in a bustling atmosphere throughout the region. As of August 31, 2023, which marked the peak vacation season, the number of daily beach visitors hit a staggering 45,482, and the influx of outsiders traveling to Yangyang on that particular day exceeded 1.6 times the resident population. This statistic underscores that when considering the "living population" - those who spend a significant amount of time or money in an area - Yangyang emerges as a more dynamic and vibrant locale compared to many other cities. So, the question arises: Is Yangyang an area marked by a declining population or one experiencing population growth?

People often claim that Seoul is expanding, but in reality, the population of Seoul has been decreasing annually. Seoul, once known as the "city of 10 million," has experienced a steady decline since its population dipped below 10 million in 2016, reaching 9.42 million in 2022. In that same year, over 80,000 individuals left Seoul, marking the highest out-migration among the 17 major cities and provinces in the country. Surprisingly, there is relatively little concern about the prospect of Seoul's decline, owing to the continuous influx of people into the city. Approximately 3 to 4 million individuals who do not reside in Seoul actively contribute to what is produced and consumed there.

These circumstances compel us to reevaluate the prevailing notions of regions and populations. A fresh perspective is imperative to overcome the looming threat of local extinction and to foster balanced development throughout the entire nation. In this era characterized by population decline, cities are undergoing a profound transformation. The traditional notion of a "fixed city," where people settle, is evolving into that of a "flexible city" which serves as a hub for diverse members of the population. The connectivity and mobility generated by a myriad of individuals are poised to become the pivotal factors determining a city's competitiveness in the future. What is required is a new paradigm that transcends the rigid distinctions between metropolitan and non-metropolitan areas or between large and small to medium-sized cities, placing a heightened emphasis on the "flow" of population between these regions.

The city is no longer stagnant; it is in a state of constant flux. New transformations are unfolding before our eyes, driven by the fluid movement of local content, people adapting to different lifestyles, and the accumulation of diverse possibilities emerging from their interactions. We propose to name cities that adapt and evolve to draw people in with their unique and inherent cultural richness and that overflow with the synergy of diverse individuals "liquidpolitan" cities. This term blending "liquid" with "-politan" conveys the idea that modern cities and regions are malleable, interconnected, and exhibit diverse transformations, much like a liquid. Through the concept of "liquidpolitanism," our objective is to capture the evolving characteristics of contemporary cities and explore fresh perspectives and methodologies for regional development. By examining the enticing aspects of liquidpolitanism, which is navigating the challenges posed by population decline, we can anticipate the future direction of urban trends.

From Settled to Liquidpolitan

To elaborate on the liquidpolitan concept, we must first delve into the notion of population, a fundamental metric for assessing an area. Population can be quantified in various ways, but historically, the "settled population" has held paramount significance. The settled population is derived from census data and represents individuals with permanent residency, forming the bedrock of demographic measurements. It encompasses those who consistently reside in a particular area at the time of the census, excluding temporary residents while including those temporarily absent.

As was said earlier, heightened social mobility has introduced new facets of population measurement. This includes the "sojourning population체류인구" – those who spend more than one night in a specific area – and the "'related population관계인구," which comprises outsiders with connections to the area. However, the concept that is currently garnering the most attention is the "living population생활인구." The living population is a novel concept that takes into account not only the settled population but also individuals who spend a specific period of time in a given area, including commuters, students, tourists, and various other groups. This population model encompasses foreign visitors on trips, daily commuters, office workers, and patients seeking medical treatment, among others. This innovative population metric was first estimated by the Seoul Metropolitan Government in 2018 and has been formalized as part of the "Special Act on Support for Declining Population Areas인구감소지역 지원 특별법," set to be implemented from 2023.

The shift from relying on the settled or registered population to the living population as the basis for this law reflects a transformative change in our perception of cities. Cities are evolving from rigid, solid structures to more fluid, adaptable entities. Even if the residential population, as seen in the case of Seoul, experiences a decline, an increase in the living population can infuse it with the vitality needed to transform into a more dynamic urban center over time. In fact, Seongsu-dong, once categorized as a neglected area in Seoul, has rapidly transformed into a trendy hotspot, attracting a young and vibrant crowd, while certain downtown Seoul areas once known as youth hubs are witnessing a noticeable decline.

If a city's foundation is built upon the settled population, it can be characterized as a "settled city." Conversely, when a city's vitality stems from the living population, it can be aptly called a "liquidpolitan city." While residential cities are the outcome of standardized urban planning that prioritizes end results, liquidpolitanism places a strong emphasis on the ongoing process of diversification and the emergence of multiple centers. Unlike residential cities that are often the product of large-scale public and local government initiatives governed by a "master plan," liquidpolitan cities are regenerated incrementally and adaptively. They come to life through the efforts of the private sector and urban content developers, who engage in small-scale experiments, fostering an environment that thrives on change and innovation.

Signature stores: Gathering places for all

The significance of a "signature store," an establishment capable of drawing people in through its unique charm representing its locality, cannot be overstated. When designing a substantial shopping complex, the renowned store that serves as a mecca of the commercial zone is often referred to as an "anchor store." In a similar vein, an appealing establishment with the power to allure individuals to a particular locale can be aptly termed a "signature store."

In Waegwan-eup of Chilgok-gun, Gyeongsangbuk-do, located about a three-hour's drive from Seoul, there exists a rural village. In this village, there's a handmade burger restaurant that manages to draw in a remarkable 80,000 visitors each year. It goes by the name "mmhs ㅁㅁㅎㅅ" (read as "mumuhusu"), a rather challenging name to pronounce.

Mmhs entices visitors to a tranquil rural village, where two-lane roads wind their way amidst unhurried tractors and rows of charming hanoks with black tile roofs. The single item on the menu that beckons them is the coveted home-made burger. Without fail, a lengthy queue forms outside the establishment, affording patrons the opportunity to take in the sights and sounds of the picturesque neighborhood while they wait. As a result, this area has witnessed a notable upsurge in its living population, all thanks to the allure of Mmhs.

The same goes for Yangyang. The role of the signature establishment known as "Surfyy Beach" has been instrumental in transforming Yangyang from what was once regarded as a depopulated area into a thriving surfer's haven. Surfyy Beach had its beginnings in 2015 when CEO Park Jun-gyu founded Raon Surfyy Resort Co., Ltd. Notably, the "Corona Sunsets Festival," organized by the beer brand Corona in 2017, is widely seen as the pivotal event that drew in young enthusiasts to Yangyang. As word spread about Surfyy Beach, surfers began converging on Yangyang, leading to the establishment of a host of surfing-related businesses and cooperatives in quick succession. It is estimated that 45% of the nation's surfing population now visits Yangyang, with 40% of surfing schools concentrated in the Yangyang area.

Signature stores are emerging as a vital component even in traditional markets. A prime example is the "365-day market³⁶⁵일장" situated within Seoul's Gwangjang Market. This establishment, touting itself as a local grocery store, stands out significantly from the traditional market stalls in terms of its appearance. The interior boasts modern design elements, featuring a vibrant green neon sign and sleek stainless steel shelves, which draw in a younger demographic. What they offer is equally trendy, ranging from natural wines to cheeses and handcrafted caramels.

In Jeju City, a similar phenomenon can be observed with the Arario Museum Tapdong Cinema. Tapdong, once a bustling city center akin to Seoul's Myeong-dong, gradually experienced a decline as government offices relocated and new neighborhoods sprang up. Notably, artist and collector Ci Kim씨킴, the chairman of Arario, repurposed an old cinema in the area into a museum. This transformation led to the emergence of brand shops, pop-up stores, and showrooms in the vicinity. As a result, Tapdong has recently earned the moniker "Jeju Island's LA," attracting a steady stream of visitors.

Indeed, small towns have garnered increased attention in recent times, largely owing to the prominence of local brands and establishments that come to symbolize their respective regions. This trend signifies a shift in how people identify with urban locales, where they become more acquainted with the names of smaller units, such as streets or neighborhoods, where signature stores thrive, rather than the broader city itself. For instance, Seongsu-dong has gained more recognition than its encompassing administrative district, Seongdong-gu, within Seoul. Similarly, people are familiar with the Gyeongui Line Forest Trail경의선숲길 but may not necessarily be aware that it falls within the boundaries of Mapo-gu.

In this context, an urban planning expert aptly expressed this phenomenon: "It feels like there are 100 Seouls within Seoul." This underscores the notion that consumers no longer perceive the city through the conventional hierarchy of administrative units encompassing city, *gu* (district) and *dong* (neighborhood). Instead, they focus on a particular area or street, driven by the presence and appeal of signature stores.

Local entrepreneurs reshaping urban landscapes

People who inject fresh vitality into their hometowns through entrepreneurial ventures can be called "local entrepreneurs." Lee Chang-gil, the CEO behind Incheon's "Open Port Road개항로 Project," serves as a prime example. In 1883, when Jemulpo (Incheon's former name) reluctantly opened its doors under Japanese influence, the encircling thoroughfare earned the moniker "Open Port Road." While once a vibrant hub in Incheon, the area's vibrancy waned due to governmental relocations and surrounding development.

Lee Chang-gil, a native of Incheon, lamented the fading allure of his neighborhood and envisioned a renaissance by repurposing aged edifices to align with modern preferences. He embarked on the Open Port Road Project in 2018, assembling a team of 15 individuals encompassing architects, landscapers, designers, planners, and restaurant staff. Their efforts commenced with transforming a former ENT clinic into a trendy café, gradually birthing over 20 unique shops and dining establishments within the open port precinct in recent years. As word spread about this transformation, businesses from Seoul, Incheon, and Songdo International Business District began eyeing the evolving opening route, leading to the recent influx of approximately 40 new establishments. Consequently, nearly 60 abandoned spaces along the open port have experienced a remarkable revival.

Kim Cheol-woo, CEO of RTBP Alliance, a city reimagination venture situated in Yeongdo, Busan, shares deep roots with his hometown, having been born and attended high school there. Historically renowned for its shipbuilding industry, Yeongdo witnessed a decline in vitality alongside the shipbuilding sector's post-global financial crisis downturn. Recognizing the need to reinvigorate the city, Kim took action in 2014 by establishing RTBP, which stands for "Return to Busan Port돌아와요 부산항에." The initial focus was on work. He introduced "Platform 135," a hybrid maker space and co-working facility, providing a haven for individuals eager to create but who lacked the necessary space and equipment. Subsequently, attention turned to leisure. A disused warehouse along the waterfront, opposite Platform 135, underwent transformation and became "GGTI끄티," a cultural hub breathing new life into the area.

Local creators connecting stores with customers

Regardless of a store's prominence or the entrepreneurial prowess of its owner, standing out in today's competitive landscape can prove challenging. Therefore, it falls upon the planner to curate an "experience journey" within a given area, driven by a keen understanding of the commercial district's unique traits and its target audience. These individuals are known as "local creators," and their covert endeavors are increasingly shaping trending locales.

An exemplar of local creation is "Urban Play어반플레이," an urban cultural content platform rooted in the Yeonhui-dong and Yeonnam-dong areas of Seoul. This seasoned urban planner initially focused on generating local content in response to local government requests. However, their collaboration with Naver gave rise to "Familiar Neighborhood아는동네," an initiative aimed at preserving Yeonnam-dong's local culture by supporting small business proprietors and creators while accumulating valuable expertise in content production.

Hong Joo-seok, CEO of Urban Play, may have a background in architecture, but his true passion lies in people rather than bricks and mortar. Notably, "Yeonhui Walk연희

걷다," inaugurated in 2015, stands out as a flagship project that propelled Urban Play into the limelight. This festival serves as a dynamic gathering, uniting local café owners, artisans, and gallery operators, all with the common goal of showcasing the vibrant spirit of Yeonhui-dong to the world. In 2018, Urban Play further solidified its status as a local creator platform with the establishment of "Yeonnamban-gagan연남방앗간" and "Yeonnamjang연남장." These initiatives underscored their commitment to fostering creativity and community within the region. Expanding their influence, Urban Play introduced the "Bound Project," a regional management model that tailors and administers customized content services, spanning from Yeonhui-dong and Yeon-nam-dong to new frontiers like Suwon, Jeju, and Gwangju.

"Glow Seoul" has emerged as a captivating urban phenomenon. CEO Yoo Jeong-soo, who initially recognized the potential for regional development through "Glow Kitchen" in Ikseon-dong back in 2015, took the plunge into urban planning with the establishment of Glow Seoul in 2018. Building upon the success in Ikseon-dong, Yoo shifted his focus to Changsin-dong, Jongno-gu. Changsin-dong, although situated at the heart of Seoul, presents accessibility challenges due to its steep, hilly terrain that connects to the Naksan Park wall낙산공원 성벽. This neighborhood has long been characterized by underdeveloped areas, with approximately 90% of its buildings classified as old. Nevertheless, the tide has turned, with Generation MZ continually flocking to the area. Young individuals, who prioritize style above all else, willingly don sneakers and scale a 120-meter-high hill for one reason – Glow Seoul's captivating spaces thoughtfully scattered throughout the residential fabric of Changsin-dong. The allure lies in the joy of meandering through alleyways, akin to a treasure hunt, where one can encounter a Chinese eatery reminiscent of a Hong Kong backstreet, or a purveyor of premium Korean donuts, or a Thai restaurant boasting a breathtaking cliffside vista.

Background of Emerging Liquidpolitanism

The emergence of liquidpolitanism is a response to the persistent decline in birth rates in South Korea. This demographic trend has led to an aging population and a concerning milestone in 2020 – the point where the number of deaths exceeded the number of births, often referred to as a population "death cross." Projections indicate that by 2060, individuals aged 65 and above will constitute half of the total population. In fact, some statistics even suggest that South Korea's population could dwindle to zero by the year 2750. In times when the population was expanding, it made sense to create new cities or execute large-scale urban redevelopment projects. This approach aligned with the increasing demand resulting from a growing populace. However, the demographic shift towards a shrinking population demands a different approach. Instead of uniform redevelopment, it has become imperative to reevaluate urban development in accordance with regional characteristics and infuse it with a diverse range of contextually relevant content.

Advancements in transportation and technology are ushering in a transformative shift in the urban landscape. The government has been diligently executing its transportation network plan, solidifying the country's connectivity. The integration of high-speed railways like KTX and SRT is seamlessly linking the entire nation, effectively shrinking the metropolitan area. The eagerly anticipated Great Train eXpress (GTX) Line A for the Seoul Capital Area is slated for a 2024 opening, and plans are underway for the commencement of construction on the GTX-B and C lines. Furthermore, preparations are in motion for the launch of the Gyeongbu Underground Expressway in 2027, with a substantial investment of 3.8 trillion won. Local governments are also expediting the enhancement of transportation networks, encompassing subterranean roadways, high-speed rail systems, and airports.

However, it is urban air mobility (UAM), also known as "air taxis," that demands paramount attention in the future. Anticipating the evolution of the mobility market from two dimensions to three, numerous companies and startups are directing their attention and investments toward the promising realm of UAM. The Korea Airports Corporation, responsible for managing all domestic airports except Incheon International Airport, has taken early steps to establish UAM standards. They are swiftly responding by engaging in the establishment of vertiports (takeoff and landing pads) and the development and operation of traffic management systems, positioning themselves as key players in the unfolding UAM landscape. Meanwhile, SK Telecom is reportedly in the planning stages of a partnership with Joby Aviation, a prominent UAM startup in the United States. Their aim is to secure competitive aircraft and introduce UAM services in Korea as early as 2025.

The development of cutting-edge, high-speed transportation represents a double-edged sword in urban planning and regional development. On one hand, it maximizes mobility between regions, expanding the range of people's activities. This helps reduce the concentration of populations in large cities and boosts domestic travel demand, thus creating opportunities for regional development. This trend is a contributing factor to the rising population in these areas. However, there are also significant negative impacts to consider. The expansion of living areas where one can traverse the entire country in half a day can inadvertently exacerbate the so-called "straw effect빨대효과." This phenomenon transforms the outskirts of major cities into commuter or bedroom towns, where residents primarily sleep and funnel their spending into the larger urban centers like Seoul. Moreover, efforts to relocate public institutions from Seoul to regional areas may become less effective. This underscores the importance of an integrated approach to regional development, one that combines the liquidpolitan concept with the expansion of metropolitan transportation infrastructure to mitigate these challenges effectively.

Finally, it's worth acknowledging the emergence of a "floating generation," characterized by their embrace of the nomadic lifestyle. This generation prefers a flexible existence, moving between various places rather than tethering themselves to a single location. As we move beyond the challenges posed by COVID-19, the debate surrounding remote work – whether to continue it or not – has taken center stage for many companies. Conflicting views on the impact of remote work on productivity have emerged. What's particularly intriguing is how Generation Z, poised to drive future changes in our work culture, views this issue. Data from the "University Tomorrow Research Laboratory for the Twenties대학내일 20대 연구소" in 2022 indicates that 66% of job seekers consider the possibility of flexible work when evaluating potential employers. Moreover, the gig economy's rise is expected to contribute to the spread of the nomadic lifestyle, as more individuals embrace freelance work. This floating generation, empowered to work wherever and whenever they choose, is poised to reshape urban lifestyles and redefine the way we work.

Outlook & Implications

100 cities should have 100 identities

Today, the concept of the "average" is fading away. Cities are now in need of tailor-made customization that reflects their unique local characteristics, rather than conforming to standardized and franchised models based on generic, average lifestyles. In essence, we must aim for 100 cities, each with its own distinct identity and personality.

Today, the individuality of each city is shining through more prominently. This means that the differences in culture and style among cities are capturing our attention. Looking ahead, consumers will actively seek out regions that align with their personal tastes and lifestyles. Just as one chooses cosmetics that match their MBTI, people will select cities to visit or live in that resonate with their preferences. Therefore, in the future, it becomes crucial to archive, meticulously manage, and safeguard the unique cultural heritage of each region. This is because a city's distinctive identity and character will become increasingly vital in shaping its appeal and attracting residents and visitors alike.

Also, the private sector's role is steadily eclipsing that of the public sector in shaping our urban landscape. The private sector, with its abundant imagination and creativity, is becoming increasingly pivotal in fostering urban diversity. To align liquidpolitanism with the evolving dynamics of our times and embrace the diversity of our population, private-led urban planning is now more fitting. While regional development has traditionally adhered to a government-led model focused on economies of scale, the current landscape necessitates greater collaboration with the private sector.

When the private sector assumes the reins in the planning and design process, it can autonomously craft the spaces it envisions and sustain them with a sense of responsibility. So, what then is the role of the public sector? It should primarily provide financial support and address various issues that may arise in the field. Additionally, the public sector needs to cultivate "trend literacy," the ability to discern shifting consumer needs and interpret trends. This entails local public officials becoming creators or marketers in their own right. Just as a company builds a brand, infusing freshness into a city demands meticulous planning, thoughtful design, and a commitment to consistent and ongoing operation. It's essential to avoid scenarios where everything, from the planning direction to the content, undergoes upheaval with every change in local government leadership or the arrival of new personnel. Continuity and stability are key to the success of urban development initiatives.

Why should we pay attention to this liquidpolitan concept? Firstly, it's essential because cities need to be adaptable to accommodate diverse lifestyles. Embracing regional diversity fosters societal creativity. In a world where industries are transitioning to the knowledge sector, the cultural capital that can offer fresh perspectives holds immense value. This is why numerous startups and IT companies worldwide place great importance on urban diversity.

Ultimately, our focus for cities should shift from asking, "How wonderful is this city?" to "How is this city evolving?" Cultivating a thriving liquidpolitan city isn't solely about revitalizing depopulated areas. It's about creating cities with expansive growth potential, rooted in diversity and creativity. There's a saying that "Innovation happens on the periphery." We eagerly anticipate the emergence of resilient yet dynamic liquidpolitans, continually experimenting with possibilities while embracing diversity and their distinctive allure. These cities hold the promise of vibrant, innovative futures.

Supporting One Another:
'Care-based Economy'

Caring is the act of providing assistance to others to help them stay healthy and alive, and the concept of care has expanded dramatically in recent years. Anyone can be cared for, even if they do not have a disability, and anyone can care for anyone, even if they are not family members. Therefore, we would like to name the new social and technological movements surrounding care the "care-based economy" as it can bring new paradigmatic economic effects in addition to welfare. The care-based economy can be divided into three aspects based on who takes care of whom and how: (1) nurturing care, (2) emotional care, and (3) relationship care. First, nurturing care refers to care that focuses on the physical difficulties of people who are unable to live alone, such as patients, the disabled, infants, children, and the elderly. Secondly, emotional care is care that goes beyond looking after physical discomfort to look after the mind. Finally, relationship care is community-based care where individuals lean on and care for one another, rather than a one-sided concept of only helping the vulnerable. Another recent trend of note is the growing role of technology. While care has traditionally been about people doing things for people, recent advances in technology have made it possible for care to be "untact," or contact-free.

It's time to look at care from a new perspective. Caring for a child is caring for a parent's career, and caring for the elderly through technology is protecting their human dignity. Taking care of your employees is an investment in the future of your organization. In the hustle and bustle of our increasingly individualized society, we all need each other's care. As an infrastructure that lifts people up and makes economic life possible, the care-based economy will become the most important economic issue of modern times with huge policy and industrial ramifications.

"The LPGA, which organizes weekly tournaments across the United States, offers a mobile childcare facility near the golf course during tournament events. This facility is staffed by three professionals with specialized childcare qualifications along with several dedicated volunteers. They use a truck to transport various equipment, including playground equipment and toys, while the interior of the facility is designed to resemble a kindergarten, creating a consistent and nurturing environment for children, even when they need to travel a considerable distance. For elementary school-aged children, there are additional programs that include exciting field trips to places like museums and zoos. Recognizing the varying schedules of the players, the childcare facility operates from 5 a.m. to 9 p.m. This support for mothers who are professional golfers not only enhances their careers but also contributes to the LPGA's ongoing success by retaining exceptional players. It's worth noting that players have often gone on to win championship trophies even after becoming mothers."

Humans, as individuals, depend on caregiving from

birth to adulthood. Longer caregiving periods often correlate with higher intelligence in species. For instance, crow chicks receive care for 4 to 6 weeks, leading to advanced intelligence and tool-using skills. Homo sapiens owes much of its success to an extended caregiving period, enabling larger brains and bodies to develop. Caring for one another is a fundamental human trait, essential for survival and the sustenance of society.

Caring involves offering assistance to those in need, whether due to their vulnerability or the circumstances around them, to ensure their well-being and health. This notion of care has evolved significantly in recent years. In the past, care primarily revolved around family members or those in close proximity providing support to individuals struggling with independent living, often due to health or age-related issues. Today, the concept of care has undergone a profound transformation. It is no longer limited to those with disabilities or specific needs, and caregivers need not be exclusively family members. Care is becoming increasingly inclusive and expansive in both social and technological dimensions, extending far beyond traditional family boundaries. This shift marks a significant change in how we perceive and practice caregiving.

As seen at the beginning, it is no exaggeration to say that one of the hidden reasons why American women's professional golf was so much more popular than other women's sports was because childcare facilities operated at each tournament site, allowing players to continue their athletic careers even after marriage and childbirth. It shows that caring for children is not just a benefit or convenience but can have enormous economic ramifications.

The care economy can be divided into three aspects based on who takes care of whom and how: (1) nurturing care, (2) emotional care, and (3) relationship care. First, nurturing care refers to care that focuses on the physical difficulties of people who are unable to live alone, such as patients, the disabled, infants, children, and the elderly. In our society's pursuit of a welfare state, this will become an increasingly important area in the future. Secondly, emotional care is care that goes beyond looking after physical discomfort and to look after the mind. Finally, relationship care is community-based care where individuals lean on and care for one another, rather than a "one-sided" concept of only helping the vulnerable.

Another recent trend to note is the growing role of technology. While care has traditionally been about people doing things for people, recent advances in technology have made it possible for care to be "untact," or contact-free. Now, depending on the type of care, let's examine the changes in the concept and its technological evolution.

Nurturing Care

It is commonly said that to gauge the quality of a society, one should assess how it cares for its vulnerable members. As the Republic of Korea, a poor country that endured colonial rule and war, went through a remarkable period of economic growth, it was determined to foster the development of the welfare state. Consequently, there has been a sustained expansion of support and care for socially vulnerable populations, and this approach to caregiving can be referred to as "nurturing care."

Nurturing care primarily centers around addressing physical deficiencies. The primary areas of focus include traditional caregiving for the elderly and children, as well as care for the sick. The trend of socializing caregiving is gaining momentum, with a growing emphasis on integrating technology into the process. With the aging population, there is a rising quantitative demand for elderly care, and with the declining birth rate, the quality of care for children has assumed greater importance. Additionally, in a society where time efficiency is a priority for everyone, there is a significant increase in demand for temporary care for sick people.

One of the most noticeable aspects is the service that matches caregiving personnel. While the aging population increases, there is also substantial growth evident in the strengthening of digital capabilities across related industries. As a representative example, the startup "Caring케어링," which provides home care services, has received praise for effectively undergoing "digital transformation (DT)" by enhancing enterprise resource planning (ERP) systems and eliminating inefficiencies that have long plagued the caregiving industry. Based on this, its corporate value was recognized as exceeding 100 billion won as of 2022, qualifying as a "preliminary unicorn." Another senior care startup, "Caredoc케어닥," set a revenue target of 15 billion won in 2023. They are expanding their business scope by offering emotional management and life care services to help seniors manage their living environment, as well as home rehabilitation exercises conducted by professional therapists to aid in recovery.

"Momsitter맘시터" is Korea's largest babysitter matching service with annual transaction volume estimated at 240 billion won as of 2022. It has received praise for digitizing childcare by connecting 400,000 parents and 800,000 babysitter members nationwide, enabling transparent information sharing between both parties, as well as convenient features such as caregiver journals and payment processing through the app. According to market analysis service Wise-App·Retail·Goods, the number of users of Momsitter's app has steadily increased since 2019 and surged until the first quarter of 2021, when various childcare institutions stopped due to COVID-19. But from the second quarter of 2022, downloads and users have been on the rise once again.

The development of "care tech" is now playing the role of replacing people with technology in many aspects of care. For example, it can help physically vulnerable people get up and exercise on their own while monitoring their physical activities. Samsung Electronics unveiled a senior-focused wearable robot called "EX1" at CES 2023 designed to be worn on the knee or ankle. It is reported that this product, also referred to as "Bot Fit," will be released with features for muscle strengthening and physical management that can be used by the general public as well.

The Korean company "Orbitn올비트앤" offers premium rollators (wheeled walking frames) equipped with remote care functions. They have integrated an AI device into the rollator to record user movement data, allowing family members or doctors to monitor it remotely. When the primary caregiver installs a mobile app and registers the device, they can view the current location of the rollator. Additionally, if the rollator goes beyond pre-defined safety zones, an alarm is triggered. This allows seniors to engage in external activities safely and independently, while caregivers can provide remote care from a distance.

When it is impossible to be by the side of people who need care, technologies that can substitute for human presence are also entering the market. The U.S. company "Care Angel" utilizes AI for voice recognition and nursing services, and also provides care by making phone calls. Every day at a designated time, the AI makes a phone call to the elderly individual and asks various questions about their sleep, health status, medication adherence, well-being, and more. It then automatically compiles their responses into a report format and shares it with family members or their doctor.

Technology also solves the problems that are essential but difficult for others to help with, such as bathing or using the toilet. Continence problems are not simply a messy nuisance but are directly related to a patient's dignity as a human being. Particularly in Japan, there is rapid growth in the technological product businesses related to addressing continence problems for people with limited mobility, including portable toilets, deodorizing products, and air fresheners. With the explosive increase in the elderly population, smart diapers are also attracting attention. Equipped with a wireless or contact-free recognition sensor, it notifies the replacement time through a smartphone app when urinating or defecating. Unlike infants who are always watched by their parents, smart diapers may be more effective for the elderly and patients who need a caregiver's help.

The field of care does not stop at introducing new technologies. Training for professional care workers is also being thoroughly conducted. The "2nd Seoul City Caregiver Welfare Improvement Comprehensive Plan (2022~2024)" announced by Seoul Metropolitan Government is a project that involves a budget of approximately 60 billion won. It aims to expand the beneficiaries of the policy, establish a specialized counseling hotline, and ensure caregivers' smooth rest and continuing education. In particular, it is crucial to note that job training on new technologies is mandatory as a way to strengthen the capabilities of care workers. This is because it is not only important to simply introduce technology, but it is also important to learn and adapt to it. In order for care technology robots or AI to be helpful to both the recipient and the caregiver, easy digital access for care workers is necessary.

Emotional Care

The most important care these days is not caring for someone's physical health but caring for the mind and spirit. We would like to call this "emotional care." Emotions cannot be controlled simply by one's will: they should be treated with the utmost care and attention, which gives one the strength to live a good life.

According to statistical analysis of depression and anxiety disorder treatments by the Health Insurance Review and Assessment Service건강보험심사평가원, from 2017 to 2021 the number of depression patients increased by 35%, and anxiety disorder patients increased by 32.3%. Especially among patients in their 20s, there was a high growth rate, accounting for 19% of the total, making it the age group with the highest prevalence rate. This may be due to an actual increase in the number of patients, but it can also be seen as a result of stressed young people actively participating in treatment. They go to the hospital to be diagnosed with their condition, receive medication to strengthen their mental vulnerabilities, meditate and keep a gratitude diary, and pursue mental recovery by sharing with others.

Emotional care for the elderly is also important. Not all old people are weak; even though they may be classified as "seniors" in legal terms, many of them are physically healthy. Although they are able to make decisions and perform on their own, they may have no place to go and suffer from a weak sense of emotional belonging after retiring and their children becoming independent. For these people, the discrepancy between their still healthy physical fitness and their narrowed social scope often leads to mental health instability. Even if they are not recipients of welfare support economically or physically, psychological care is necessary. As a result, various solutions are being devised to take care of their minds.

The Daekyo Group, known for its education service for children and teenagers, began a senior life solution business called "Daekyo Newif대교뉴이프" in January 2022. By applying the know-how and knowledge accumulated as a children's education company to new audiences, they are now offering a wide range of services covering the entire life of the elderly population, such as operating a nursing care training center, training and dispatching professional instructors, and developing cognitive enhancement content.

The number of day care centers for the elderly, so-called "Seniorgartens" (senior + kindergarten노치원) is also increasing. In the way preschool children use childcare facilities such as daycare centers and kindergartens and receive government support, this system provides care for the elderly during the day. For example, "Please Take Care of Mom엄마를 부탁해," a senior care center located in Songpa-gu, Seoul, allows admission to seniors over 65 years of age who are classified as "long-term care" individuals. They offer tailored programs for seniors, including indoor sports like throwing balls, silver cognitive sports, music therapy, art therapy, recycling crafts, and outdoor social activities. Every morning, they drive around nearby residential areas to pick up elderly individuals, provide lunch and snacks, and offer medication guidance if needed. Basically, they provide daycare. From the perspective of the elderly, it is fun to meet peers, talk, and spend time doing various activities appropriate for their age while being safely cared for. And it is popular for families because they can continue their individual lives, such as going to work, doing housework, raising children, and pursuing leisure activities.

The method of using AI speakers to alleviate the loneliness of the elderly and enhance their sense of self-efficacy has already become common. SKT's "NUGU" smart speaker system has a "sentiment word dictionary" with 2,400 entries in the "emotion category." It analyzes the speech of elderly users who interact with the speaker and detects four emotions: depression, loneliness, well-being, and happiness. Through this, if it is determined that they may have emotional difficulties, it provides psychological counseling or connects them to local government services. In addition, KT and Naver are also operating "AI Speaker Care Service" and "Naver Clova Care Call," respectively, for the elderly. For seniors who live alone and have difficulty coping with situations quickly, various services are provided, such as becoming a companion to alleviate loneliness, engaging in conversations for dementia prevention, and sending SOS emergency rescue requests in urgent situations. In fact, there was a case where an elderly woman living alone, who showed symptoms of cerebral infarction in the middle of the night, said "help me" to the AI speaker, which immediately called an ambulance that saved her life.

Robots also play a similar role. The "Parental Love Hyodol부모사랑 효돌" doll, also known as "Hyosun효순," is an AI robot playing a 7-year-old grandchild. Developed by the Hyodol Company, the doll's main body is equipped with various sensors, and it responds with its voice when touched. Even elderly people who do not have high tech literacy can use it just by patting the doll's back, holding its hand, or hugging it as if they were interacting with their grandchild. This doll gained popularity as local government offices began actively introducing it to alleviate the loneliness of elderly people who found it difficult to go out due to the spread of COVID-19. As of July 2023, there are approximately 7,500 seniors in Korea who use Hyodol.

The recently increasing number of reclusive adolescents is also a subject of attention. Lately, a new branch of cleaning services has gained prominence: cleaning the rooms of reclusive adolescents. "Gwangju Metropolitan City Reclusive Loner Support Center광주광역시은둔형외톨이지원센터" is Korea's first public institution of its kind. One of the items in their "Healing Program" is room cleaning. They not only engage in conversations with reclusive adolescents to help them express their inner thoughts but also clean up accumulated trash in their rooms. Through this, they aim to instill a sense of self-efficacy by cleaning up their neglected lives. It's a way of caring for the hearts of adolescents through cleaning.

Another development in emotional care is clothing products for people with developmental disabilities. The smart vest "HUGgy허기" from social venture DolbomDream돌봄드림 (literally "Care Dream") is a piece of clothing that utilizes the "deep touch pressure (DTP)" effect to provide a feeling of security, as if someone is hugging you by applying appropriate pressure to the human body and stimulating parasympathetic nerves. They took the idea from life jackets and applied the air injection method to create casual clothing that can be worn in everyday life. A vest monitors the wearer's emotional state and stress levels based on their physiological information and automatically inflates air accordingly. HUGgy users experienced a 28% increase in class participation at school, a 57% reduction in stress, and even students who had difficulty writing a single line during class were able to concentrate enough to write about two pages. Furthermore, the time it takes to fall asleep has also decreased, allowing for more effective care of individuals with disabilities through emotional means. Hugging brings emotional stability to the mind and body, and it has various positive effects on bodily functions. The CEO of Care Dream, who developed HUGgy, said that they will expand their services, not only to people with developmental disabilities, but also to the elderly and the general public who have little interaction with others.

Relationship Care

These days, the lives of ordinary people are also becoming common focal points of care. It's not because they need care; it's simply about relying on one another as fellow humans.

The commonly used term "care gap돌봄 공백" is not only an issue for infants or the elderly. Anyone who has to live in the fast-paced and hectic "time-efficient society" can become a recipient of care. Therefore "relationship care" is being widely applied and evolving into a social agenda that local communities are interested in together.

The "Milk Greetings우유안부" campaign from Maeil Dairy delivers milk every day. If milk accumulates in front of one household, a certain score is given to determine whether the household is at risk. Delivery drivers or neighbors are often aware of the situation and take action first, notifying government offices which will lead to appropriate and stable care.

Convenience stores that are open 24 hours a day are also expanding their presence as beacons of relationship care. Convenience store CU has been playing the role of a precinct station for local communities since 2017. A report button connected to a pre-designated police agency is affixed inside the payment booth or on the card payment terminal, so it can be easily pressed in an emergency. Through a co-operative security effort between convenience stores and the police, it has established itself as part of a neighborhood's safety network by providing emergency protection for lost or abused children and facilitating quick reporting in case of criminal threats. Many local governments are also utilizing convenience stores to look into any blind spots in care for single-person households. Yeongdeungpo-gu in Seoul has strengthened promotional activities with residents through cooperation with local convenience stores to identify crisis households in welfare blind spots. In addition, Gyeong-gi-do's Dongducheon City has implemented policies in collaboration with local convenience stores to identify low-income households facing food shortages due to economic difficulties or experiencing overall crises.

Recently, there have been cases where neighborhood cafés or independent bookstores serve as a communal space for residents of the local community. "Bo Market보마켓," located on the first floor of Namsan Mansion in Hannam-dong, Yongsan-gu, Seoul, is a "lifestyle-oriented neighborhood supermarket" that sells daily necessities, serves as a snack bar, and aims to create a friendly atmosphere like a cozy village café사랑방. It's a place where children can have a snack after school or academy while they wait for their parents, or even where people can enjoy a birthday party for a dog – everyone is welcome. It is a local community that thoughtfully reflects the context of the neighborhood.

Within companies, there has been a growing movement to actively care for employees' lives and family relationships. Continuous employee care has led to improved productivity and competitiveness within companies, making it recognized as one of the survival strategies for attracting and retaining talent. Counseling programs are also essential requirements. To enhance the sense of stability within organizational relationships, companies have introduced various programs such as "therapeutic trips힐링 트립" for employee training (LG Energy Solution), "counseling talk concerts마음 상담 토크 콘서트" (Hyundai Motor Group), active operation of in-house counseling centers (SK Innovation's "Harmonia," SK Hynix's "Mind Stroll마음산책"), and meditation programs that take care of employees' "mental gardens마음 밭" like "Talk Terrace" (Kakao). BGF Retail, which operates CU convenience stores, has introduced an online counseling program as part of its employee assistance program (EAP) to improve accessibility to counseling for its employees. "Hanwha Systems" has expanded psychological counseling support to immediate family members, while Lotte Construction has made counseling available to employees, their spouses, and children.

Organizational care know-how within a company can also be spread to local communities or customers. Lotte Department Store operates a counseling center called "Rejoice" at four branches, including Centum City and Jamsil. They provide quality counseling to local residents or customers at reasonable prices, offering programs that encompass all generations, including art psychotherapy and child intelligence testing. They also collaborate with social welfare agencies nationwide to provide specialized psychological counseling for low-income and vulnerable populations. In 2022, they took care of the daily lives of 286 participants in 10 welfare centers across the country. All of these can be considered cases where both businesses and communities have cared for each other.

Public institutions are also presenting specific measures. With rental scams becoming a significant social problem and many young people suffering due to a lack of information related to real estate contracts, public care policies related to this issue have since emerged. Seoul has been providing a free "single-person household rent safe contract assistance service1인 가구 전월세 안심계약 도움서비스" since the summer of 2022, which has received praise for not only assisting single-person households but also benefiting the real estate contract system. By thoroughly preparing to ensure contracts processed safely for real estate customers, and by being able to guarantee the quality and trust of transactions, the real estate industry is also positively contributing to the establishment of a transaction order that was not easily improved upon in the past.

Outlook and Implications

The origin of the word "care" is the Old English "*caru*," which means, worry, sorrow, anxiety, and grief. "Caring" means looking after the vulnerability of a living organism, but it also has the dual meaning that facing the fragility of life can be challenging and cause much anxiety and grief. From August 2022 to July 2023, emotional word analysis related to terms like "caring돌보는" or "care돌봄" over the past year also clearly reveals this dual meaning. The positivity rate of related words is 66%, while the negativity rate is 34%. Expressions of satisfaction with care actions or services such as "good좋다," "happy행복," "love사랑" are evident, but there are also expressions of laboriousness in various aspects such as psychological, physical, and financial challenges, with the terms "burden부담" and "difficult어렵다."

Care is an economic issue

Caring is increasingly being recognized for its economic value. Caring is becoming the foundation that protects everyone and enables a better life in our slowing economy, contributing as a crucial pillar to the economic cycle, driving the force of new economic growth, which can reflect on GDP. The economic value generated by care is clear. Care targets people rather than goods and focuses on reproduction rather than production. Usually, we refer to the foundational elements that enable economic activities such as roads or power grids as "infrastructure." In that sense, care can also be considered an economic foundational element because caring for the daily lives and minds of members of society and helping the vulnerable is the foundation for more active economic activities.

In fact, recent care services are the key to facilitating economic activities. In 2023, the health and welfare sector has seen an increase in the number of employed people, which Statistics Korea attributes to the growing demand for care. Looking at the steady number of employees in the health and social welfare service industry (148,000 in April 2023; 166,000 in May; 126,000 in June; 145,000 in July), even as employment growth has slowed down, it can still be seen that care services have become a key field leading the economic cycle. In the venture investment industry, which has been shrinking due to the interest rate hike in 2023, the majority of companies that attracted an increased investment amount were mainly care-related and life-oriented startups. For example, platforms like "Caring," which connects caregivers with the elderly, and "Tictoccroc제깍악어," a service that matches childcare teachers with infants and children, have each attracted investment of 30 billion won and 16 billion won, respectively. This indicates a positive outlook for the care service field.

Care within the family is also recognized as having economic value, rather than as private help. According to a study conducted by the UK insurance company SunLife, the care provided by grandparents, assuming they look after their grandchildren for an average of 8 hours a week, would have an annual value of £4,027. Since 2011 in the UK, when grandparents take care of grandchildren under the age of 12, they can extend their pension period by up to 5 more years, increasing their overall pension, and thereby preserving the economic value of caring for grandchildren. In some local governments in Japan, "grandchild leave" is also possible. If parents are busy, grandparents can also take time off to look after the children.

Seoul Metropolitan Government has started a service that provides 300,000 won per month from September 2023, where parents can entrust their child to a relative such as a grandparent or a first cousin. It has converted grandparent childcare into market prices. Also, if parents qualify for a certain grade of long-term care insurance and their sons and daughters hold a caregiver qualification, they can receive home care insurance benefits재가요양보험금. The fact that sons and daughters can receive financial support from the government even if they care for their parents at home means that the economic value of care is recognized.

I need care, too

It's time to adopt a fresh perspective on care. Taking care of children is akin to safeguarding parents' careers, and employing technology to assist the elderly is a way of pre-serving their human dignity. Providing care for employees serves as an investment in the future of the organization. By empathizing with one another, people with disabilities can coexist within society, and when one's neighbors feel at ease, one can also relish more comfortable days.

The socialization of care extends beyond the mere relocation or commercialization of caregiving activities from inside the home to outside of it. It entails acknowledging that anyone can be both a giver and a receiver of care. A truly inclusive social capacity for care exists when the concept of caregiving is integrated seamlessly into the daily lives of individuals, irrespective of their gender or social status.

To do so, the duty of care should not be limited. There is a need to expand the legal definition of "family." In the 2021 "National Awareness Survey on Family Diversity (Ministry of Gender Equality and Family)," 68.5% of 1,500 citizens aged 18 to 79 cited "sharing of housing and livelihood" in addition to "marriage and blood relations" as requirements for a family. In the National Assembly Legislative Office's report, "The Reality and Policy Challenges of Family Diversity: The Necessity of Recognizing Non-Relative and Close Relationships" published in May 2022, recognizing the possibility of mutual care and support among individuals who share their livelihood as close relationships was argued for.

Internationally, the scope of family members considered for care is already being expanded to include "those who are as close as family." In the U.S. states of Colorado, Connecticut, New Jersey, and Oregon, "a person that the worker shows to have a close association with … which is the equivalent of a family relationship" counts as a family member covered by paid family and medical leave laws, and in Washington, the wording is expanded to include "any individual where the relationship creates the expectation that the worker care for the individual and that individual depends on the worker for care." In Sweden, people can receive care allowance from the government if someone cares for a "close relative" who is suffering from a serious illness, and this includes friends or neighbors. In this case, "as long as the worker considers them as a family member," they can become eligible for caregiving. If they can provide appropriate assistance in situations where another individual needs care, such as illness or an accident, those individuals are considered family.

The impact of caregiving has a ripple effect. Those who receive proper care are better equipped to provide quality care to others, forming the bedrock for improving the over-all well-being of society. We all have caregiving roles, and we all deserve to be cared for in return. The phrase "a mother also needs a mother" emphasizes the universal need for help-ers and caregivers in our lives. Care isn't merely assistance. Indeed, care is a personal matter, for someday we may find ourselves the ones in greatest need of care services.

2024
Consumer Trend Insights

초판 1쇄 발행 2023년 11월 14일

지은이 김난도 · 전미영 · 최지혜 · 이수진 · 권정윤 ·
　　　　한다혜 · 이준영 · 이향은 · 이혜원 · 추예린 · 전다현
감수 미셸 램블린
펴낸이 성의현
펴낸곳 미래의창

등록 제10-1962호(2000년 5월 3일)
주소 서울시 마포구 잔다리로 62-1 미래의창빌딩(서교동 376-15, 5층)
전화 02-338-6064(편집), 02-338-5175(영업) **팩스** 02-338-5140
홈페이지 www.miraebook.co.kr
ISBN 978-89-5989-720-9 13320

※ 책값은 뒤표지에 있습니다.

15세 미만 구독 불가

마학의 패왕과 과법의 총희 1~2권

키나코 모치즈키 지음 | Nardack 일러스트 | 이진주 옮김

과학이 쇠퇴하고 마법이 「마학」이라 불리며 발달한 세계.
그곳에서는 「복음」이라 불리는 주문과 같은 기술이 사회기반이 되었다.
과거의 사건을 계기로 마학을 싫어하게 된 평범한 고등학생, 아이바 하지메는
문부마학성의 엘리트 나학술사, 미사키 미우를 만나
전세계에서 「마학」을 바르게 쓸 수 없게 되는
「복음모순」이라 불리는 현상이 일어나고 있다는 사실을 알게 된다.
「복음모순」은 400년 전에 근절당한 과학—
「과법」을 신봉하는 「과법술사」가 일으켰다고 한다.
하지메는 지금의 세계에서 마학을 바르게 사용할 수 있는
유일한 인간일지도 모른다는데……?

검희와 총희가 번뜩이며 춤추는
신세대 마법과학 배틀 액션 러브코미디!

©Tatematsuri/OVERLAP
Illustration Ruria Miyuki

신화 전설이 된 영웅의 이세계담 1~5권

타테마츠리 지음 | 미유키 루리아 일러스트 | 송재희 옮김

오구로 히로는 일찍이 알레테이아라는 이세계로 소환되어
《군신》으로서 동료와 함께 나라를 구하고,
주변 나라들을 정복하여 거대한 제국을 건설했다.
그 후, 히로는 모든 것을 버리기로 각오하고
기억을 잃는 대가로 원래 세계로 귀환한다.
그 후, 매일 행복한 날을 보내던 히로는
무슨 운명인지 또다시 이세계로 소환되고 만다.
그곳은 바로— 1000년 후의 알레테이아?!

자신이 이룩한 영광이 「신화」가 된 세계에서
「쌍흑의 영웅왕」이라 불렸던 소년의 새로운 「신화전설」이 막을 올린다!